finding Elizabeth

True Stories of Comfort for Grieving Hearts

L. Shannon Andersen, M.Ed., LMHC
Bereavement Counselor

With Reflections by Elizabeth Palin

Dedication

To the children

*To Elizabeth Palin, for all the work she does
to help educate and heal our broken hearts.*

*A special thanks to all the courageous parents
who shared their stories here in hopes of helping other
families and loved ones through their journey of grief.*

Contact L. Shannon Andersen

To book Shannon Andersen for
events, conferences or
other services call
1-386-503-0380

For more information about
Shannon and her other
publications, go to
www.TheMagdaleneAwakening.com

Finding Elizabeth

L. Shannon Andersen

Table of Contents

L. Shannon Andersen

℘ Introduction ℘

I started working with hospice in 1999 and that began my sincere personal exploration of death. There is nothing like facing the reality that at some point in the future we will experience the death of people we love to bring us face to face with that truth, except, that is, the actual death of someone we love which makes the experience considerably more poignant. In 2002 the only deaths in my life were at a distance.

When my grandmother died at 89, I began to ask questions and seek answers for myself. Raised with a traditional Methodist upbringing, I found little comfort with the answers offered within that tradition. I explored further and sought clear proof for myself that she survived the death of her body and found that comfort in my own experience of what has been called After-Death Communications. I tell that story in the first chapter of my previous book *The Magdalene Awakening*. The chapter is called 'The Lily.'

Through my work with hospice the losses in my life accumlated. Most difficult were the deaths of children, and more particularly young people for whom I cared. It was those deaths that brought me to this project.

For some, the places I go to in this book are threatening to their Christian faith. For that reason I have left out some parts of my personal story in order to honor their wishes. However, what I have learned in this experience has only strengthened for me what I learned from my Christian faith, the message of Jesus: life is eternal. For me the story I am recounting is a testamony to that truth and the proof I sought. What I have learned brings me comfort and faith in the reality that our consciousness survives the death of our body and that in fact 'we don't die.'

❧ Foreword ☙

The Question of Death

"Those who learn to know death, rather than to fear and fight it, become our teachers about life."
Elisabeth Kubler-Ross

Every culture in human history and all religions across time have attempted to understand the great question of what happens after we die. Is death merely a doorway to another dimension or the final end of our existence? In the past the reigning scientific view held that there was no such thing as a soul and that consciousness was a function solely of the brain; but today even science has begun to expand its parameters and has joined the quest with an opening mind.

When exploring this immense question we must ask ourselves: has science and the scientific method offered us an adequate picture of reality? If the scientific approach has been too restrictive in its call for the use of the scientific method and double blind studies grounded in the material physical world, then we have to say some remarkable things have been revealed in the history of metaphysics and religion, which may not have been acknowledged with deserved respect.

Dr. Elisabeth Kubler-Ross, an internationally known expert on death and dying and a pioneer for hospice care, was a renowned individual who explored deeply the question of what happens after death. Part of her early work on grief was recorded in her book *On Death and Dying.* She wrote that book for professionals dealing with grieving individuals.

On Death and Dying was just the first of more than 20 books she would write. It was based on the real lives of the 500 terminally ill patients Kubler-Ross interviewed. In it she said, "Many relatives are preoccupied by memories and ruminate in fantasies, often even talking to the deceased as if they were still alive." The inference is that the relatives were living in a world of fantasy in order to cope. In her later work, however, she began to investigate the idea of survival of consciousness and, after exploring near-death experiences, she made a conscious and dedicated decision to address the question, "Do we, in fact, survive the death of the body?"

By her account, almost immediately people began to come to her with their stories of proof. Story after story provided her evidence that the human body is merely a container and our consciousness survives bodily death.

Near the end of the 1970s, she became interested in mysticism, which included her own spirit guides, and as a result came to wonder if death existed at all, or if death was no more than passing into another world. She was also one of the major pioneers in the investigation of the near-death experience. Twenty years prior to the publication of Raymond Moody's book, *Life after Life,* she recorded numerous near-death experiences.

The Spiritualist Movement, through mediumistic communication, has long addressed the question of what happens after death. In this movement's study, it appears that there were certain individuals who, after they died, felt they needed to stay around in an attempt to help us understand the nature of this phenomenon of death.

The movement is usually traced to the Fox family who gained notoriety in the 1840's, and it flourished in the early 1900's both in the United States and in England. It was a wing of the Christian Church. Though fraught with a reputation for trickery and fraud, there were those who had incredible gifts of the Holy Spirit and whose good faith and effectiveness as mediums has never been successfully challenged in spite of rigorous investigation.

In America, Edgar Cayce, a dedicated Christian man who taught Sunday School his entire life and read the Bible through once a year from the age of 9, was called the sleeping prophet. He founded the Association for Research and Enlightenment (A.R.E) in Virginia Beach, Virginia. His messages from the trance state began to provide answers to questions about health and to enlighten those who sought broader spiritual knowledge. Many of his 20,000 readings included answers to the question of what happens to us after death.

Around the same time in England, Arthur Conan Doyle, primarily remembered as the famous author of Shelock Holmes novels, became one of the leaders in the Spiritualist Movement. After his sons died in the war, he found comfort through the messages he received through mediumship. He himself came back after his death with a message through Grace Cooke, a gifted medium of her time. That story is recorded in a book first published under the title *The Return of Arthur Conan Doyle.* Grace Cooke later went on to found the White Eagle Lodge in England, now a world-wide organization that continues her work today with the purpose of bringing comfort to the grieving.

It is surprising that, in an American religious culture firmly based on the belief that life survives the death of the body, there would be nay-sayers to the idea that our loved ones who have died might be willing, anxious and able to bring a message to those they love from across the veil.

Many believe they themselves receive evidence of the survival of their loved ones through what Bill Guggenheim, author of *Hello from Heaven*, calls After-Death Communications (ADC's). Guggenheim has written about the experience of 300 of the 10,000 bereaved people he interviewed while researching his book on the survival of consciousness. Those 300 reported having their own 'contact' from their dead loved ones. These ADC's came in a variety of ways.

Today more and more people have been looking for "proof" of life beyond death. The need for an answer to the question becomes more intense after the death of a loved one; and seeking talented intuitives, psychic mediums or receivers of communication 'from beyond,' has become more popular and acceptable since the advent of television programs like John Edward's prime time shows and the wave of other popular television programs on the same or similar topics.

Historically, mediums have received bad press because of a few frauds, and many people associate mediumship with séances and drawn drapes. Today there is a new movement afoot and the drapes are pulled back. People such as John Edward, George Anderson, Sylvia Brown and James Van Prague are accepted in mainstream Christian homes.

In fact today those who have this talent will most likely tell you that you too can develop your own intuitive abilities. Psychic medium communication is like tuning the receiver on a radio. There are of course different skills and different levels of skill associated with this gift and there are factors that affect a clear communication including, as Edgar Cayce pointed out in his readings, the motivation, doubts and attitude of the person receiving the reading. However, just as with any other talent, a few people have exceptional skills. I was lucky enough to meet one of those people in the winter of 2002. Her name is Elizabeth Palin.

Elizabeth falls into the category of exceptional. Her skill as an "intuitive psychic" enables her to act as a conduit for those who have left their bodies behind. Her gift to those who have passed over as well as those to whom she brings their message is one of hope, healing and knowledge. On a personal level, I am someone who has sought the answers to the question of death and survival of consciousness; and was called upon by life to reaffirm my belief in life beyond death when I too experienced the loss of a loved one. Elizabeth came into my life at that time, and since then I have interviewed numerous people who have helped me come to the inescapable conclusion that there is a place and at times a genuine need for people such as Elizabeth Palin on the journey through grief and loss of a loved one. That conclusion propelled me to write this story.

In my professional as well as my personal life, I view the soul as the very essense of our being so I see it as a priority in working with clients who hold the same beliefs. The death of a loved one brings each of us to our knees to question every thing we've ever believed and during times of grief spiritual questions are at the forefront.

The grief journey is a long and often dark road to travel, but for those walking it there are many ways to cope. Exploring spiritual questions is a part of the journey. As I have worked with the grieving, I have learned that if it is within the belief system of the bereaved there is a place for the transpersonal view by taking into account the fact that there is a much bigger picture than we can know from our traditional limited perception. In fact, to leave the spiritual aspect untouched in an interaction of grief counseling with its tremendous resource for healing is like taking a scalpel away from a surgeon. The topic might be left untouched if the counselor is uncomfortable and/or feels it is inappropriate to address.

Grief and death always require us to ask ourselves the great questions of life and we all have to find our own answers. For those who are open, there is evidence - some would say proof - that consciousness does not end when we leave our bodies. I see our loved ones willing to provide us with the comfort of knowing the truth, whether through direct After-Death Communications or through talented people such as Elizabeth Palin. I am enormously appreciative of her skills and of the comfort she has brought to my family and me, and to many others whose lives she has touched.

Elizabeth Palin is a fascinating, marvelously gifted individual. The story of how she entered our lives unfolded in uncanny synchronicities. At the start of the millennium, far too many young people died in tragic deaths in our small community. As a grief counselor, I was asked to help facilitate a 'Parents in Mourning' group for many of these families, never dreaming my heart would soon be broken by the death of my daughter's friend, who died tragically in an accident.

Seeking more comfort than our group could provide, one family found the services of Elizabeth Palin in an extremely uncanny way. In the chapters describing this encounter, you will hear how this strong young spirit came through unexpectedly to a friend of his fiancée, begging her to bring his family to see Elizabeth so he could communicate with them. As you might imagine, word of this amazing occurrence spread quickly throughout our community; and, one by one, many of the families touched by tragedy were soon comforted by the loving, healing heart of Elizabeth Palin.

In the chapters that follow, the families share their magical stories, sometimes in their own words, sometimes as told to me in conversations. Miraculous transformations fill these pages. After finding Elizabeth, people find peace and comfort in the knowledge that their departed loved ones are always near and continue to have a blessed, fruitful and happy life after life.

After each story, Elizabeth too looks back over her encounters with the young ones who so tragically died, yet who so valiantly fought to cross the thin veil in order to communicate with their parents, siblings and friends. During my interview with Elizabeth in Part II, she also relates some of her own life story, and gives intriguing answers to questions about her work. Finally, in Part III, parents report on their own After-Death Communications from their children.

If you are drawn to this book, chances are you too have had a loss of a loved one, perhaps even the loss of a child. I pray the following true stories will bring comfort and peace to your grieving heart.

〜〜〜〜〜〜〜Reflections by Elizabeth〜〜〜〜〜〜〜

* For parents whose children have died *

Even though I constantly work with death and with those who have died, it continues to amaze me that loved ones who have died can successfully convey messages through me. Over the years I too have doubted, but I have been convinced through evidence over and over again when I receive specific names, thoughts, and images. It has taken me a lifetime of working with the spirit world to know and understand that we truly are spirit and there is no death, only a transition to another plane.

As for me, I no longer question. Proof has been provided by those on the other side. They are my teachers; and I am so happy to have been able to provide for them a link to the ones they love, the ones left here. Most of all, I feel so blessed to be able to add comfort and hope for the parents and family of those who bless my little room. It is my hope that these stories can bring comfort to all who read them.

Elizabeth Palin

〜〜〜〜〜〜〜〜〜〜〜〜〜〜〜〜〜〜〜〜〜〜〜

Dear Elizabeth,

I can't thank you enough for the messages you brought to me concerning my daughter who had recently passed over. I have been living in turmoil since this has happened and your messages brought peace, love and happiness to me. Thank you for giving me the answers I have been searching for. I left you feeling content and happy.

Jan Myatt

ରେ Part I ଞ

The Young Departed

~ Elizabeth Palin ~

Chapter 1

Finding Elizabeth

I sat in a wicker chair, hands twitching in my lap. The pale yellow porch was adorned with bright flowers and broad shuttered windows open to the light. When the middle aged woman stepped through the door leaving the small apartment on the lower level of the ocean front house in Flagler Beach, Florida, our eyes met. She had just finished her session with Elizabeth.

With little hesitation I asked, "Was it a good reading?"

"Incredible!" she said.

"Did you have a loved one come through?"

"Yes," she said, tears now forming in her eyes, "It was my son."

"How long ago did he die?"

"It's been two and a half years," she responded, tears now streaming down her cheeks.

"I'm so sorry," I offered automatically. "I'm a grief counselor. Though you can't compare grief, I know there is nothing harder than losing a child."

"You never get over it," she said, her head rocking in a fashion to bring emphasis to her statement.

"Never, I know that is true," I responded, "but somehow you can learn to 'get on with it,' without their physical presence," I said.

"What does a grief counselor do?" she asked.

"Well," I hesitated, trying to synthesize my thoughts, "A grief counselor listens, and allows you to talk about your loss, express your feelings, and, probably most importantly lets you know what is normal. Of course, nothing about grieving seems normal. Many say they feel as if they might be going crazy. People often can't sleep or eat, or they sleep all the time and can't stop eating. They say they can't think, focus or concentrate. The pain comes in waves, and the days, weeks and months move with a roller coaster of emotions. There is no timetable for grief; it takes as long as it takes.

All experience grief in their own way and in their own time. As you must well know by now, eventually the pain that first feels as if your heart is literally being stabbed eases, and the feelings of loss soften. You are right, you never get over losing a loved one, and, even though you should never compare your grief to another person's, from my experience there is no greater loss than the loss of a child."

"I've been doing this for a number of years and I've seen people begin to live again, but it usually takes longer when it's your child. I know people can learn to move forward if they are willing to do the emotional work that grief requires. I've had my own experience with grief, and worked with so many grieving people, I know that life can continue, though at first it doesn't feel like it."

"Coming to Elizabeth helps," the woman continued. "Having a reading with her is reassuring. When I leave, I really feel that he's okay. Elizabeth knew his name and everything. She knew so many details, things there is no way she could have known. She's amazing! It really does help, but it doesn't keep me from wanting him with me."

"Yes, I know," I said. "She helped me too. I had a loved one die ten months ago. He was like my son. I cry every day and carry his picture with me. I still miss him and want him to be here, but I know he's fine."

"With Elizabeth's help, I've come to know that now we have a different form of a continuing relationship. Of course, we all have to come to our own knowing and we all have our own beliefs. When I experienced the loss, I questioned everything I thought I knew. Finding Elizabeth helped me confirm my belief that our loved ones are still with us. They'll be waiting for us when we pass over. I also realize there is so much more than we can understand with these limited bodies and minds. Our departed loved ones become our teachers; their death becomes a course in life; and grief becomes our curriculum. By their dying, they can teach us that there is a much bigger picture, if we are open, that is. They can still teach us from beyond their bodies about the bigger reality of who and what we really are."

Our Story Begins...

I was standing in the kitchen when my husband read the story from the 'Flagler Times' aloud, but I had no idea I knew the young man who had died in the tragic motorcycle accident. I just shook my head in despair and said, "We've lost another young person."

I hadn't seen Jody, the young man in the accident, in five years, and at the time did not remember I'd known him as a client.

In my work as a grief counselor, my own life had of late been touched by many tragedies but, most recently, tragedy had struck close to home. A number of my daughters friends and classmates had died, including one very special friend who we all loved.

I too was struggling. How could this happen? I asked myself over and over again. There was nothing about these deaths that made sense. For Melissa who had lost so many friends and for me, the world seemed to turn black. Nothing I offered my daughter seemed to help, and because of that I felt helpless.

I knew what I believed, or at least I had a foundation to stand on. I had spent my whole life asking those important questions about life and death, not leaving a stone unturned in the quest for understanding the "bigger picture." I was raised with a strong Christian foundation in the Methodist church. I later studied world religions, psychology, philosophy, and metaphysics. I knew what I believed about death. For me, death was no more than stepping through a curtain. I knew that within myself...but my daughter was only 17. How was she supposed to understand? She still questioned and how would she feel comfort? I was desperate to help her, but, knew I could not be her counselor. She refused all of my efforts to send her to grief counseling. She would schedule and then cancel appointments.

This was the state of our lives when I received a call from a friend, Stacy. Stacy Grein's 16-year-old daughter, Shannon, had died in a tragic car accident almost exactly a year before. Shannon went to school with my daughter Melissa and they had mutual friends. Stacy called to tell me about Jody Cass.

"Yes," I said, "I read about it in the paper. I can't believe we've lost another young person."

The rash of deaths among young people in our small community continued. I had in recent months been asked to help facilitate the Parents in Mourning group, and my heart ached for the families of those young lives taken by trauma. Never had I found a more difficult dimension to my work.

In my job, I most often deal with the grief of people who have lost loved ones with a terminal illness; however, watching young people die traumatically was different. Coming face-to-face with the loss of children tore my heart out.

After the first Parents in Mourning group, I went home and clutched both my kids. My son Treve was 18 and Melissa was 15 at the time. I knew how fragile life was and I would lie awake whenever they were late. My heart would go to my throat whenever the phone rang at night.

It was not long after I started to help with the Parents in Mourning group that Shannon, Stacy's daughter, had been killed while driving with a group of friends on the way to a party. She was sitting in the back seat and she was not wearing a seatbelt. My daughter Melissa was supposed to have been with them that night. That had made Shannon's death even more personal. I knew it easily could have been Melissa who died in that accident.

At the time Stacy called to tell me about Jody, she wondered if I could do anything to help his mother. At the time I knew only that Jody was the brother of Jessica, who had grown up with Shannon and attended school with Melissa, my daughter. Because of Stacy's request, I called to offer my condolences to Carol Larmore, Jody's mother. Through Carol, I met Windy, Jody's fiancée.

The first time I met Windy, a beautiful young blonde woman, she showed me a picture of Jody on his motorcycle. At that moment I knew I recognized him but I couldn't remember how.

Windy told me about their accident. She had been on the back of that motorcycle and had sustained a terrible head injury and facial wounds. She lifted the hair off her forehead to show me the fresh red scars on

Jody Cass on his 'bike'

her temple. She was wearing a neck-brace.

"I don't want to cry," she said. "It really makes my head hurt when I cry. I try not to cry." She told me the story of the accident and she told me something else. She said that on Thursday of that week she was going to do something she'd never done before. She was going to see a psychic/medium in Orlando.

"A friend of mine went for a reading last week," she said. "In the midst of her reading the psychic told her that she had a blonde friend who was in a motorcycle accident. The woman then described our accident and what went on at the scene. She saw people there who arrived prior to the ambulance. She said they were covering us with blankets. The psychic told my friend that Jody was there at the reading and that he wants me to come. He wants to communicate with me. I'm a little nervous. I am hopeful. I am looking forward to it. I've never been to a psychic before. This is really strange, but I'm going."

I wished her luck and asked her to call me and let me know what happened. I too was really curious about this woman in Orlando. Could she really be communicating with Jody? When I saw Carol, Jody's mom, she had given me Jody's picture, which I took home with me to put on my altar. She called it his "Smile Face" picture. After meeting with Windy I looked at it carefully. He looked so familiar. *How did I know him*? I asked myself. I knew his mother's last name and at that moment I was assuming his last name was the same as hers.

When we met, Carol told me a number of stories that had brought some comfort to the family. One was about a little boy who came up to Jody's brother in a supermarket and handed him a small book called *Joey Goes to Heaven*. Another was about someone who had seen a man at a conference who looked just like Jody, and when he walked up and introduced himself, it turned out his name was Jody as well. A third story was about one of Jody's siblings meeting someone at a hardware store with Jody's first and last name. Carol found meaning in these occurrences, feeling they were 'messages' from Jody. Through the stories I learned Jody's full name. His name was Jody Cass.

I often talk to those who have passed over to let them know I'm listening and praying for them and their loved ones who are missing them. *Let me know if I can help I'm listening for your guidance*, I had said in a whispered prayer that day. I had two impressions. One was a comment he made about his stepfather that would later prove true. The other was the image of fringe coming out the end of some handlebars.

The next day I went to a doctor's appointment and had a lot of time on my hands to sit and think. I was quite disturbed by Jody's death and the pain his family was encountering. I kept feeling I knew Jody, but somehow it just wasn't coming together. I thought about the images in my mind…the fringe on the handlebars…the little book called *Joey goes to Heaven* that Carol had told me about. I wondered why it seemed so relevant when she called him Jody, not Joey.

All of a sudden, I knew why. They called him Jody, but I'd known him as Joseph! I DID know Jody. He had been involved in an accident and I was his vocational rehabilitation counselor. I had seen him for about 6 months. I had been very fond of Joseph (Jody!). In his own way he was very charming. He'd come a long way to get his life together, and, at the time of his death, he owned and ran his own architectural design company, designing homes for the area's well-known builders. He was so well liked, that when a model home designed by Jody was completed, it was named "The Jody" in his memory.

Once he had come to a street dance to help out with the youth. I was remembering the last time I'd seen him. It was there. He'd ridden up on his motorcycle. He was wearing his black leather jacket. I remembered that his jacket was unique. It had long leather fringe along the bottom of the sleeves. It was the fringe I'd seen in my mind when I'd first opened up to Jody in my prayer. Now, I too felt the full impact of Jody's death. I called Carol immediately from the doctor's office on my cell phone.

"I knew him," I said. "I was his Vocational Rehabilitation counselor."

"I remembered Jody talking about you." Carol said. At that moment, it felt as though he was orchestrating something. It seemed as if he was bringing us together. I believe that was soon to be confirmed. Jody, Carol and Windy were about to help my daughter Melissa and me with our grief and our understanding of a much bigger picture. They were about to lead us to Elizabeth Palin, the psychic in Orlando. Windy called after her reading to tell me she had met with Elizabeth and that the experience was transformative. She gave me Elizabeth's telephone number. I called right away.

~ ~ ~

Elizabeth Palin lives in a community just outside Disney World called Celebration. When I called I was not expecting to get an appointment any time soon. It was the week after Christmas and I was surprised to find she could see us in a few days, before the New Year. I scheduled an appointment for Melissa and me. I also scheduled a session for Priscilla, who had been in the car with Shannon, Stacy's daughter, and for Priscilla's mother, as well.

~ ~ ~

Melissa was not sure how she felt about going, but, I had great hopes she would find comfort. I was not disappointed. Elizabeth met us at the door and let us in. Melissa was the first to enter Elizabeth's "little room." When she came out we pulled her aside with a notebook in hand. "See Mom, I told you I'd be alright. She knew so many details. She knew his name, how many brothers he had. She said his father met him on the otherside. She saw me standing with him at the service and putting the note in his pocket. He said he was with me when I was cleaning my room last week and he even knew I'd gotten three purses for Christmas. Mom, she said he will always be with me, like a guardian angel and that I will be fine."

I was so grateful Elizabeth had been able to bring Melissa the reassurance she needed and the reassurance I needed as well.

~~~~~ *Reflections by Elizabeth*~~~~~

* *For Melissa* *

Melissa, a young vibrant girl came with her mother Shannon. She'd lost a friend she loved in a car accident and was having a difficult time. She was devastated and her mother was so worried about her.

Melissa came in first. I felt a presence. I heard the name and she confirmed it. The information flowed and I was able to give her evidence...the evidence she needed to hear.

I told her he was safe and he did not suffer. He wanted her to know everything was fine. He was with his young friend, Shannon, who had died in an accident too. They were together in spirit. Neither one of them was wearing a seatbelt when they died in the accidents.

As I write this I'm getting a message for their friends and other young people. They say, "Please don't think you can get away with not wearing a seatbelt!" They also said they never believed anything would happen to them and they want their friends to know it can!

He wanted Melissa to be happy, as happy as he was when he was with her. He said they will always be with her; they will always be in each other's heart in life and in the beyond.

The day Shannon Andersen and her daughter came to visit me for a reading, I had no idea it was a part of a bigger picture. How could I have known so many young souls from the community she lived in had made their transition to the other side? Some of their friends and families had already been to see me, but at that time I didn't know they were connected. In the months and years that followed, other young ones from the same small community would tragically die. Incredibly, as time passed, they would all cross paths, in life and in death.

Through me, these young ones who had passed made sustained efforts to contact their loved ones. By providing me indisputable evidence of their continued existence, they were doing their best to get messages of healing and comfort to their families, as well as warning messages to their friends about driving, suicide and drugs in hopes that their miraculous messages would reach more than just a few. Their persistent callings have driven me to get their stories - their messages - out into the world.

తతతతతతతతతతతతతతతత

❧A Historical Perspective ❧

Sir Arthur Conan Doyle on Spiritualism
Notes from *The Life of Sir Arthur Conan Doyle*
John Dickson Carr

Arthur Conan Doyle was the famous author of the Sherlock Holmes mysteries but he is not as well known for his last crusade: spiritualism. In a biography *The Life of Sir Arthur Conan Doyle*, John Dickson Carr described the Spiritualist period of Conan Doyle's life as his last battle. According to his biographer, many thought Conan Doyle had "lost his emotional balance or mental grip" because of his passionate support of spiritualism, but Carr goes on to report the event leading up to that mission and what happened during Conan Doyle's crusade.

On October 21, 1916, Arthur Conan Doyle's article was published announcing his belief in communication with the dead. With a background of interest and belief in spiritualism Doyle proclaimed he had just entered the most significant mission of his life. At the end of WW I he lost his son Kingsley, and shortly thereafter his other son Innes died. Their deaths and his grief fueled his mission. His wife completely supported him. For the rest of his life he traveled all over the world to give free lectures on life after death and spiritualism. For this he was severely criticized losing many of his friends. Nonetheless, his lectures continued.

He said, "From the moment that I had understood the overwhelming importance of this subject, and realized how utterly it must change and chasten the whole thought of the world when it is wholeheartedly accepted, I felt, ...that all other work which I had ever done, or could ever do, was as nothing compared to this." His message; "They are not dead."

Following his six-volume history of WW I he was to devote all of his time and energies to the cause of Spiritualism.

He wrote *The Vital Message,* and *The New Revelation.* After receiving messages from his two sons at Merthyr in Wales he said to his wife, "My God, if people only knew—if only they could know!" With heartfelt determination he resolved to take the message with his own voice to every corner of the world.

He said, "I cannot do anything else. All my life has led up to this. It is the greatest thing in the world." Loved by so many and supported by so few, his biographer noted, he "girded on his sword for the last great fight of all."

For a strenuous 11 years he traveled and lectured. He would speak anywhere, challenging his opponents. For him it was a question of what he had to do. He started his lectures with:

"I want to speak to you tonight on a subject which concerns the destiny of every man and woman in this room…" During the years of traveling he wrote his book *Wanderings of a Spiritualist.* In the early 20's he toured Australia and America speaking to packed houses. As sometimes happens when Christians disagree, they accuse those who think differently from themselves of being in cohoots with the devil. To one such accusation Conan Doyle replied:

"In all ages those who disagree upon religious matters have endeavored to show that their opponents were associated with the devil. The supreme example, of course, is that of the Christ himself, Who had this charge leveled against Him by the Pharisees, and Who answered that 'by their fruits you would know them.' I cannot understand the mentality of those who attribute to the devil the desire to prove life beyond the grave…"

~ Jody ~

Chapter 2

Jody's Story ~ A Message in a Bottle

Windy nearly lost her life in the motorcycle accident that killed her fiancé, Jody. She was unconscious when the helicopter took her to the hospital and found out only later that 32-year-old Jody had been killed. Just engaged, they were very much in love, but love is something that lives forever, transcending death, and Jody, her lost love, reached out to her, through Elizabeth.

Windy's message is an amazing tale:

My friend had gone to see Elizabeth and I remember it was shortly after my accident. I hadn't really said a lot about what I was feeling. She had lost her father and that was the reason she was going to see Elizabeth. She was also interested in her romantic life and just general questions about her life. Around the same time I had been trying to reach her. Something was telling me I needed to talk to her. So, I called her.

When she answered the phone, she said, 'Oh, my gosh, I just got back into town, and I was just about to call you!'

'I was feeling miserable. The timing couldn't be better.' She said, 'I just went down to see Elizabeth Palin, the psychic I was telling you about.'

I said, 'Oh you did?'

And she said, 'No, No, No, you don't understand! I've got to tell you this. Jody came through!'

I couldn't believe what I was hearing; I said, 'What? Don't even joke, that's not funny.'

She said, 'No, No, he really did.'

I couldn't believe it, I said, 'What did he say?'

She said, 'No, I have to tell you the whole story. Elizabeth started talking to me and she said, 'There's a young man coming through. He's showing me that he passed in a motorcycle accident.' I was sitting there and not putting two and two together because I had come about my father and my love life. So I said, 'No, I don't know who you are talking about.'

And then Elizabeth said, 'There's a person with blonde hair in your life.' I thought, I don't date any guys with blonde hair, I don't know who she's talking about. This is a mystery because I don't know who she's talking about. Then Elizabeth started to describe the crash site...and I got it. All the hair on my arms stood up!

I looked at Elizabeth and asked, 'Tell me something. Is this person with blonde hair a male or a female?'

Elizabeth said, 'Oh, female my dear. These two people loved each other very much. He has a message for her. He said to tell her yes, he knows how much she loved him, and not to feel guilt over the accident. She has nothing to feel guilty over.'

Those were the two things that I had been agonizing over. Elizabeth gave my friend the answers to the questions that had been going through my head over and over again. I wondered if he knew, even in his last moments, how much I loved him and I had felt such tremendous guilt over the accident. It was just amazing to me that Jody could come through Elizabeth and my friend so that I could get his message.

My friend insisted that I make an appointment, which I did right away. I was really nervous. I had never been to a psychic before in my life and I didn't know what to expect.

When I walked in, Elizabeth said, 'Oh what happened to you?' I was still really beat up and I was wearing my neck brace.

I told her, 'Oh, I was in an accident.'

Elizabeth said, 'No, but you weren't alone.'

I said, 'Oh?'

She said, 'No, he's here.'

I sat down and started shaking and she immediately continued talking about him without a word from me. I just started to cry. She just knew everything. She described the accident and told me things about the scene that I didn't remember.

Jody began to talk to her about the birthday that was coming up. That was his sister's birthday. She then told me he knew I had started moving furniture.

I asked, 'furniture?' I couldn't think what

she was talking about and then I remembered. We had just moved the bed from my house to my mother's house because I was staying there so I could rest easier.

She said, 'Jody doesn't like that; he wants that bed moved back to the house.'

She told me things that were just amazing. It was just amazing! Jody had messages for me to deliver to his mother and his family. It brought me so much peace. I have gotten so many messages from Jody through Elizabeth. It was so nice to know that he was there watching over me and his family.

My aunt who had died was there in the reading as well and there were other people there too. My stepfather Bill who had died only a couple of months before the accident came through for my mother too. It had been a difficult time. Bill came through in my later readings with Elizabeth as well.

Jody's and Bill's deaths, and meeting Elizabeth, have turned into an amazing spiritual journey. I can't tell you how much it meant to me to find Elizabeth. Well, what I should really say is that I am really grateful that Jody found Elizabeth, and that she was able to help bring us back together even after his death.

~ ~ ~

Almost four years after Jody's death, Elizabeth, Carol (Jody's mother) and Windy (Jody's fiancée) met to talk for a video Elizabeth was making to document their experiences.

Elizabeth recalls:

I remember this young beautiful dark-haired girl (Windy's friend) came to see me. All of a sudden this young man came in, a spirit, and I said, 'Who is Jody?' I was seeing a "J" over his head. I could see his fiancée with a neck brace still on. I told the young woman, he wants his fiancée to come. He has something he wants to tell her. I could see that she was still beating her-self up; and he seemed to want her and everyone else to know that he was okay.

Windy:

Jody proposed to me right around my birthday in September and he did that with a message in a bottle. You have to understand that Jody did not have a romantic bone in his body. He was a motorcycle rider, this tough guy. He was just not romantic, so for him to do this was simply out-of-character. He had his sister plant this message in a bottle on the beach and as we walked along, I picked up shells.

When I saw the bottle I said, 'Look at that! Let's open it.'

He said, 'No you can't read it now, you have to wait.'

I said 'Wait? Why would we wait?'

He said, 'Oh, you can't read it here. You have to take it up to the house'...and that is how he proposed.

It was magical and wonderful, and really, as I said, out-of-character for Jody.

Jody and Windy - Jody proposed with the 'message in a bottle' just over one month before his death.

Carol (Jody's Mother):
To tell you how Elizabeth came into our lives, I go back to October 19, 2002. Jody and Windy had come out of the restaurant. It was late. He lived less than a mile from that restaurant. They took a shortcut through an unlit parking lot.

Windy:
I was behind him on the motorcycle, and we went by one cement island, but there was another island right by it. We couldn't see it and the bike went down. We hit the other island. He died instantly and I was rushed by helicopter to the trauma unit. I didn't know until the following day that he had died.

Carol:

I was scared. For the first time in my life I didn't know where my son was. Windy tried to tell me that she felt he was still around. She tried to make me believe there was a way he could let us know, she gave me books to read but I wasn't reading them. Then one day she called me, hysterical, and she said, 'Jody got in touch with us! Jody got in touch with us.' I didn't know what she meant. I thought she had lost her mind.

Windy:

Only to my family had I said, 'Do you think he knows how much I love him? I just feel such tremendous guilt over this accident. Do you think that I did something to cause it?'

So when my friend went to Elizabeth, she said 'there's a young man coming through.'

Carol:

She (the friend) was there to get a reading about her deceased Dad, and, as she's sitting there for this reading, Elizabeth said, 'Who's the blonde? Who's the blonde? I have a young man coming through. He's very strong, and he wants to see her. They were in an accident.' She started describing the accident scene, the motorcycle and everything. Then it hit this young woman that she was talking about Jody and Windy.

Windy:

Elizabeth said, 'He's insistent. He's showing me he died in a motorcycle accident.' My friend said all the hair on her arms stood up and on the back of her neck.

Carol:

The important thing to note is that this woman was not close to Windy at that time, they were just working in the same office.

Windy:

My friend looked at her and said, 'Tell me something...is the person with blonde hair male or female?'

Elizabeth said, 'Oh, female my dear; these two people loved each other very much. He has a message for her. He said, 'Yes, he knows how much she loves him and not to feel guilt. She has no reason to feel guilt.'

Carol:

Jody came through saying, 'I need to speak to her. Tell her I'm sorry and yes I still love her. It wasn't her fault.' She needed to hear that.

Windy:

I have to tell you that I felt such tremendous relief, because I couldn't say goodbye to him. I had been sitting for weeks just staring off into the distance because I loved him so much and I can't tell you what relief it gave me. There's no way she could have known.

Carol:

The most important thing was that when I was getting up to leave, she held me back and said, 'Your son is saying, 'Stop counting the children, I am still your son, you still have five."

That was amazing because no one in my

family knew how distraught I was, how I ached to know how to answer the question, 'How many children do you have?'

I want him to be my son here, but if he has to be there, I still want to count him. That was significant because that had been in my thoughts the night before I went to see her. She was exactly what I needed...she was like a shot in the arm...I can't imagine Elizabeth not being in my life.

⁖⁖⁖⁖⁖ *Reflections by Elizabeth* ⁖⁖⁖⁖⁖

* For Jody Cass *

Last year a young lady came for a reading. I started the reading and then I felt the presence of a young man. He filled the room with so much energy! He wanted to make me aware of his presence. I told her he was showing me an accident scene and that there was a motorcycle involved. He showed me his girlfriend with blonde hair who was hurt very badly. He spoke of his love for her and his love for his mother. He showed me a big family and let me know they were all struggling with their grief. It was hard for them to keep on going.

His death had left the entire family devastated. I felt his urgency, "Please let them know that I did not suffer." I felt an overwhelming love from this young soul. His name was Jody, and over the many months since his death, he provided messages to help so many members of his family who were living the pain of his death. He especially sent a message that day to his girlfriend Windy; he wanted her to come. She was able to get his message from her friend and soon Windy, and Jody's mom, Carol, showed up on my front door step.

~ ~ ~

⋆ *Windy* ⋆

It was some time ago, but, I can still remember when a young woman came into my room. She was wearing a neck brace and had a terrible facial injury. Walking right beside her was Jody. He was giving her messages of comfort through me as soon as she sat down. His mother came in after and he was there for her as well. Jody was such a strong presence and I did not know that he would be the one to bring together the families and loved ones of other young ones, some who had already passed and others who were yet to die.

I can see them now. They are all working together on a special mission of healing. They are encouraging their families on this side of the veil to continue to get their messages out.

Some of the family members on this side use the Internet and websites, some do training and seminars, some fight for legislation and change, some educate both adults and young people with their message to help save lives. These young people and their families are on a mission of love to help prevent young deaths and to help ease the pain of grief. It seems they would like to prevent others from suffering the pain of loss, but also, they want to bring comfort to the grieving.

They want people to understand the full reality of what death is and that even after death life goes on. Sometimes in my work I get weary, but, I remind myself of the faces of the young ones that come into my room. I remind myself how their families leave with hope and appreciation. I remind myself how much lighter they feel and once again thank God. I say, "Thank you God for the wonderful work you've just done through me and thank you for choosing me to do this work." Then I am renewed and experience the gratitude for the wonders of my life.

જાજાજાજાજાજાજાજાજાજાજાજાજાજાજા

I have had the pleasure to have three consultations with this glorious lady and would like to say that she has been an inspiration to me and I am completely amazed each time I meet with her. She has a gift that has made my life much more fulfilling and peaceful - a gift for reaching people that have passed from this life and making that loss turn into an understanding that helps one to cope with such a loss. She gives hope and positive reinforcement. She is a compassionate person who you can tell is truly compelled to help everyone she touches.

Until my first consultation with Ms. Palin I had been to only two other consultations in my 50 years of life. I look forward to my next visit and hope she will remain here. She is a blessing.

Angie Parker

~ Shannon ~

Chapter 3

Stacy and Shannon Grein

Stacy shares her story:

My life was forever changed on April 9, 1998, when my sister Janet died. Her death was sudden and completely unexpected. With it, a spiritual path opened up that I could never have predicted. In order to cope, I began to read anything I could get my hands on that had to do with the survival of consciousness; anything that could give me evidence that life continues after death. I read book after book about the spirit world and mediums; books about George Anderson, James Von Prague, and Sylvia Brown.

At one point, some of the members of my family and I were able to go to see John Edward when he came to Florida. We were in the gallery and he singled us out. He said that Janet, my sister, was with her childhood friend, Denise, and her nephew, Eddie. It was incredible, but at the time I didn't know I was being prepared for another loss. The hardest loss anyone could be asked to endure.

On September 23, 2000, my whole world stopped. My 16-year-old daughter, Shannon, was killed in an automobile accident. Because of my sister Janet's death, I was no stranger to mediums and the comfort they could offer, and was quick to seek help. I was, and am still, so thankful that Jody, Carol's son, brought Elizabeth to us.

Carol told me about her reading with Elizabeth and I immediately called for an appointment. Driving there I was very nervous. I was really afraid that Shannon might not come through. I asked myself; how would I feel if she didn't? But there was another part of me that knew it was going to be great. I would hear from Shannon.

My husband Pete and I went into Elizabeth's reading room first. Connie, my sister, and her husband Sal waited outside. Elizabeth was so welcoming, her peaceful nature helped to calm me.

Elizabeth said, 'There are a lot of young energies who have passed around you.'

She then began talking about a young boy, which disappointed me, because I, of course, wanted to hear from Shannon first. Later, I realized the boy was my nephew, Eddie, who had already come through after his death in a reading with John Edward.

Then she said it: 'There's a young girl who passed in an accident. She had long blonde hair.'

That was Shannon!

Elizabeth said, 'She passed fast. One moment she was here, and the next she was gone.'

She said at first Shannon was confused because it had happened so fast. She told us there were five kids in the car and one of them was a male (true). And she said that Shannon was the only one who died (true). She even knew that Shannon had been in the back seat.

Elizabeth told us Shannon was glad none of her friends were hurt and she wanted them all to go on with their lives and to be happy.

Then Elizabeth said, 'You have her hair' and pointed at my purse. I hadn't even told my husband Pete! I had a locket of her hair tied with a pink ribbon in my pocketbook.

She said she saw Shannon dancing with a long white dress. I was so happy, because Shannon had taken dancing lessons for 10 years and she loved to dance. Whenever I see Shannon in my mind, I picture her dancing in a long white dress. It was one she had worn in one of her recitals.

Elizabeth then asked if she had had an open casket.

I said, 'Yes, she did.'

At that point, Elizabeth said Shannon told her it was okay, that she looked okay. When Elizabeth told us that, it answered a question I had asked only myself. I wondered, 'Did I do the right thing?' Was it okay with Shannon that we had chosen to do that? I had always worried because they tucked her shirt in and I always thought Shannon would have hated that.

Elizabeth then told us that Shannon tormented the cat and her little sister. That made us laugh, that certainly was true of Shannon.

Then Elizabeth said, 'I can hear guitar music. Who writes the music?"

Before we could answer, Elizabeth went on, 'Shannon says she helps her brother write the music.' At the time, Shannon's brother Pete was in a band and he wrote the lyrics to most of the songs they sang.

Elizabeth said she saw Shannon's dad and 'the little one' (MacKenzie, Shannon's little sister) fishing. 'Shannon loves to watch them fish,' Elizabeth said. MacKenzie was 7 or 8 years old at the time and she always wanted to go fishing with her Dad.

Then Elizabeth said she saw me with pictures all around me. 'Your daughter likes the scrapbooks.' When Shannon was alive, I did a lot of scrap booking, and Shannon loved the results.

Then my sister Janet came through. She said Janet and Shannon were together and that Janet was really a lot of fun, and she was! When my sister Connie and her husband went in after our reading, Janet stepped forward. I think Janet sat back and let Shannon spend time with me. Janet knew that I needed that, but Janet really came through for our sister Connie when she went in for her reading.

We were all amazed by the experience. How could Elizabeth know so much? The other amazing thing was that when Elizabeth talked, she used Shannon's mannerisms and expressions. In a later reading she said Shannon said MacKenzie was so lucky because she had gotten an IPOD and for no good reason! MacKenzie had talked her Dad into buying it for her, and it wasn't her birthday or a special occasion!

When Elizabeth talks about Shannon, often she runs her hands through her hair, exactly as Shannon used to. Another thing was she knew that the police officer brought me Shannon's watch, and I told him it wasn't hers. I knew it was, but I think I was in shock. Elizabeth said Shannon told her, "Duh, Ma," and then Elizabeth hit her own forehead with the butt of her hand. "It WAS my watch!" It was exactly what Shannon would have said and done. Shannon was letting me know with the same mannerisms and expressions that it really was true! Elizabeth is amazing!

Over the years, whenever I've had readings with Elizabeth, Shannon seems to know exactly what I'm doing in the house, such as when I was redoing the kitchen, or buying new dining room furniture. She even knew details right down to the color of the upholstery.

Elizabeth has been able to bring us such peace of mind. We know Shannon is still with us and she knows what goes on in our day-to-day lives. We are also reassured knowing that we will all be together again one day. I am so thankful for Elizabeth as she has helped us to form a new kind of relationship with our children and loved ones, a relationship that continues.

Shannon dancing in her white dress

Shannon's dancing career started early.

Flagler Palm Coast High School Dance Team

∽∽∽∽Reflections from Elizabeth ∽∽∽∽

* For Shannon Grein *

Yesterday, while doing my readings in the same community most of the young people lived in, a young girl in spirit stayed around throughout the entire day. She was there for the first and second reading. I kept thinking, "Why are you still here?" She felt so light and bright and then I heard her name, Shannon. When my third reading came in and she was STILL there, I was really confused. I said, "You didn't know Shannon too, did you?" Then they said "Oh yes, we knew Shannon."

She was full of light and giving me the impression that she was at peace and reaching young souls. She was dancing in a spotlight, just as she used to do while she was alive. If she'd only worn a seatbelt she might still be here dancing.

She handed me a pink rose. I have a prayer card of Saint Teresa whom I love. It says, "St. Teresa, pick me a rose from the heavenly garden and send it to me with a message of love." So, many times in the spirit communication I receive, those from the other side give me roses for their loved ones. Sometimes they give me a bouquet, *and sometimes just a special one, like Shannon's pink rose. Roses, roses, roses...I can even smell their scent. I thank God for allowing me a glimpse of the peace and tranquility on the other planes of consciousness.*

❧❧❧❧❧❧❧❧❧❧❧❧❧❧❧❧❧❧❧❧❧

Elizabeth has given me hope. After losing my daughter three years ago, I have been on a mission to find out everything I can about the spirit world. In doing so, I've read many books on mediums and their readings for the grieving, especially grieving parents. I found that in England there are so many gifted mediums. English people are open to believing that contact is possible – according to my readings.

When I heard of an English medium in Florida I was elated. Elizabeth certainly did not disappoint, matching the expertise of any of the mediums I have read about. The reading I had with her was superb! She reached my daughter telling me facts that only I knew. She also gave me messages from my parents and friends. It was a healing experience and Elizabeth is outstanding as a medium. We are so fortunate to have her in our country.

Frances M. Oglesby

~ Randall ~

Chapter 4

Leona and Randall

Soon the word began to spread in our community, and other parents who lost a child were finding their way to Elizabeth. Leona's 18-year-old son, Randall, died May, 2003 of an accidental overdose of the prescription drug, Oxycontin.

She and her husband had tried 11 years to conceive Randy. He was their world. The devastation his death caused both of them is beyond words.

Elizabeth had actually predicted Randall's death several months prior to his overdose.

Leona's story:

After I had my first reading with Elizabeth, I called my stepdaughter, Randall's sister, to tell her what Elizabeth had said. I was really shocked to find out she knew all about Elizabeth. In fact, she had been to her a number of months before my son Randall died, and in her reading, Elizabeth had foretold Randall's death!

Randall's half sister had gone to see Elizabeth, but I was unaware of it at the time. She lives in Orlando not far from Elizabeth and word gets around about Elizabeth in Orlando. When she went to Elizabeth, Elizabeth told her that someone in the family was going to die in May of 2003 and that the name began with the initial 'R.' Well, Randall's sister was taking care of her Uncle Ray and he was very sick. She assumed it would be her Uncle Ray who would die. As it turned out, it was her brother, my youngest son Randall.

When I called her she said, 'Oh my Goodness, she predicted Randall's death! I thought it was Uncle Ray she was talking about. I never would have dreamed it was Randall!' It was hard for all of us to believe.

When I went to Elizabeth my daughter was with me and the first thing Elizabeth did was make a fist in front of her own face. I didn't know what she was doing.

She said, 'This is for you.' Then she opened her hand and said, 'Your son is giving you a rose.' The last gift that Randall gave me was a single rose on Easter. That confirmed for me that he was with us that day.

Then she said, 'He's showing me a rosary.' Well, there was a rosary. When Randall was laid out, my mother put my grandmother's rosary in his hand. Everyone assumed it was done by the funeral home. It was never mentioned. Nobody talked about it, but Elizabeth said Randy was giving the rosary back to his great grandmother because he didn't want it. It was my grandmother's rosary and Elizabeth said it was my grandmother who met him when he crossed over. That was amazing because nobody knew about that, only my mother and myself!

Elizabeth said he wanted to thank me

for fixing his hair because he didn't like his hair either. He said it wasn't right. When the people at the funeral home fixed his hair, it really wasn't Randall. They had it all pushed back and he had beautiful dark wavy hair. I told my mother, 'Do something, fix it, do something with his hair. That's not Randall.'

She did. She went and got a cup of water and wet his hair and it just curled right up. Elizabeth said he was thanking me because he hadn't liked his hair either.

Another thing was his jacket. He had a black leather jacket that he had gotten from his father at Christmas. It had the name of a band he really loved on it. Elizabeth said he wanted to know what happened to his jacket. The day he died, that very night, one of his friends came over and his father gave him the jacket. That was very confirming.

My husband saw Elizabeth as well. He saw her with my granddaughters in a group. He said that when she started Elizabeth had led them in a meditation. In the meditation he could see Randall standing with a hat by his side, and then in his imagination he saw Randall put the hat on his head. When the meditation was over, Elizabeth came right to him and she said, 'There's a young man standing right next to you and he's got a hat by his side and he's putting the hat on his head.' My husband broke down because he knew our son Randall was there.

Then Elizabeth went on to ask him about shoes: 'Are you wearing Randall's shoes?'

My husband said no. His feet were bigger than Randall's. He couldn't wear his shoes. Then she went to my granddaughter and asked if she had a new pair of shoes. She kept saying, 'There's something about shoes.' At the time, they didn't know what she was talking about. We didn't figure out what she was talking about until he came home and we were discussing it.

What had happened was that about the time Randall died, my husband had been expecting a pair of shoes from a catalog. They never showed up. The post office said he had received them, but we never got them. We tore the house apart looking all over for those shoes. I even looked out in the garage, but I couldn't find them. The company was just about to send him a new pair of shoes, and I just happened to be out in the garage, cleaning up.

I found a box I thought was empty, but when I pulled it out and looked in, there were the shoes. That's when we started to figure it out. In April when Randall was still alive, he must have been going out somewhere when the postman delivered the shoes. Anything that had the name 'Randall' on it Randall considered to be for him even though he was named after his father. He must have opened the box and when he saw they weren't for him, he must have thrown the box in the garage and taken off.

So, that was the story about the shoes. He'd forgotten to tell his father about them and he obviously wanted to let us know what had happened through Elizabeth. That proves Elizabeth wasn't just reading our minds, which of course you wonder. The real story of the shoes was something we didn't even know! Randall solved the mystery after he had died. Only he knew the whole story.

Then Elizabeth said he was asking my granddaughter why she wasn't wearing his shirt. He told her he liked it when she wore his shirt. That day she was planning to wear Randall's shirt, but was afraid it would upset her grandfather so had changed her mind. Elizabeth also told my granddaughter that she saw him pulling her hair, which he always used to do. Elizabeth was right about everything.

Everyone loved Randall's smile.

Randy loved contact sports early in life.

Randall at his high school graduation.

Randall and his grandfather - their last picture.

❧❧❧❧❧ *Reflections by Elizabeth* ❧❧❧❧❧

* *Randall* *

An 18-year-old boy, very handsome, a good boy, died of an accidental overdose of a prescription drug Oxycontin. He's the one who just urged me out of bed. His message was, "Please don't forget. It's so important." The words keep running through my head. He tells me there are so many young people who are experimenting with that deadly drug. He wants me to tell them of the devastation the use of that drug can cause. He wants me to tell them it robbed him of his life and it broke his family's heart. So much grief for the people left behind. I asked him, "Randy, what message do you want to send?" He said, "Elizabeth, tell anyone who's tempted not to do it! Have the courage not to do it!" His parents work with a group to help educate people about how deadly Oxycontin can be when abused. They recommended the website:

www.Oxyabusekills.com

❧❧❧❧❧❧❧❧❧❧❧❧❧❧❧❧❧

~ Stephanie ~

Chapter 5

Valerie and Stephanie

Valerie tragically lost her 22-year-old daughter, Stephanie, to suicide. Stephanie, a beautiful and talented athlete and scholar, was Valerie and her husband Terry's only daughter. Stephanie's death changed their lives forever. Out of her despair, Valerie visited Elizabeth two and a half years after Stephanie's death.

Valerie tells her story:

> *Life is difficult. We all have pain but losing a child has to be one of the worst things anyone could experience. I now say I'm not afraid of anything else that might happen. The worst thing that could ever happen has already happened. Visiting Elizabeth was just one way I chose to try to survive the pain.*
>
> *I first heard about Elizabeth at our Parents in Mourning group. We had gathered on a Sunday to share our grief and find support. We all (there were seven of us mothers who had lost children) brought food for lunch, and sat and talked about our experiences and coping with the deaths of our children.*

One mother had lost her son in a motorcycle accident only seven weeks before. She told us of her trip to a medium in Orlando and how her son had come through loud and clear. She was skeptical at first but said that there were too many unusual things that only she knew. One thing she told us about was that the medium said she had been looking for her son's watch at the crash site. Her son came through and told her the watch had flown off his wrist in the accident and someone had picked it up.

There were several other things she mentioned as well. The medium's name was Elizabeth Palin. I didn't know whether I should go to see Elizabeth or go back to see another medium I'd seen the year before. I also had a friend who wanted to go with me. I had hopes that I would hear from my daughter, Stephanie, who had died two and a half years before. Joe had hopes of hearing from his son.

Three of us from the Parents in Mourning group went to see Elizabeth: Joe, myself and one other parent who did not wish to be included in my story. Joe and I share the common bond that our children took their own lives.

It was on Friday, January 3, 2003. She lived in Celebration, which is the Disney planned development where the big houses are very New England looking, with large front porches.

On the way over Joe talked a lot, as he does. I enjoy him so much because he reminds me of my mom's family - vivacious and sincere. He is so emotional but says he is doing better coping with his son Sydney's death. He talked on the way over about not getting back all of Sydney's clothes and especially his shoes. He was very upset about the shoes the police didn't return to him. The other parent reminded him that they probably had to bag everything up as a precaution and then threw it away. Joe was very distressed, as he wants everything from the day his son Sydney died.

Anyway, we got to Elizabeth's house and I was the first to go in, as we had drawn straws. She was very pleasant and I sat next to her at a small table. She looked over my shoulder, as if she saw someone in the background and started talking. She said she saw a woman she thought was my mom sending me her love and wanting me to know she was very tired before she died, but now she is back to the way she was before she was ill. My mother had died after an extended illness.

Elizabeth saw a lot of women friends around her. I said that it was not my mother but was probably my mother-in-law. Elizabeth said that my mother was there also, and that they both are okay...that they both passed from an illness but that one was quicker than the other. That was true.

Then she saw two children and asked if I had children who had passed over. I said one, but she insisted there were two there, a boy and a girl. I said I had a miscarriage and she said that was the boy, and that his life here was not meant to be, but that he is still very real and that he is now my guardian angel. She said that he would reincarnate.

She asked who was a Gemini and I said that was my Dad. She saw him in the background and said he was staying there, letting all the women go first. She asked if I was Catholic because she could see my Mom holding up rosary beads. That too was true! I had been raised Catholic and still treasure my faith.

Then she said that Steph was with both mothers (meaning both her grandmothers), and that she loved them and had been with one longer here than the other. She asked how Steph passed and when I told her she had taken her own life, she said that she was too sensitive for this life but that she has a lot of life now. She said there was no pain when she died - that the only pain is the one in my heart. She said there was family waiting for her when she crossed over. She is with animals and children and is a teacher on the other side. She said Steph is also helping people here with emotional and substance abuse problems. She said that I have more empathy now.

She asked if I was doing talks and lectures. I told her that my husband does, and that I often write the words. She said that Steph is helping with that and that she is pleased about the words. She is determined and trying to help from her side.

It was so cute because she started playing with her hair and said that she could see Steph wearing her hair in all different styles and colors and asked if she had ever dyed it bright red, which she had at one time! There was one short period that Steph had dyed her hair truly red! She saw her pierced ears and then made a wavy motion with her hand and said that we had had "quite a time" with her.

She said Steph knew I was coming because I had talked to her about it. I sure did! I talked to her all the way to the session asking her to be there. Then she asked who was a Libra. (I couldn't think right away but now know it's my sister-in-law.) She said she is having difficulty emotionally and that her mother is trying to get through to her and that she needs someone to help her.

I then asked a question about the journaling I'd been doing. I had been transcribing Steph's journals and responding with my own words. I asked if Steph was okay with the idea of publishing it someday. Elizabeth quoted her as saying, 'That would be great - that anything to help other people is the thing to do.' She said that Steph's death was a cry for help and that Steph hadn't understood her own emotions.

Stephanie with her parents, Terry and Val

She turned a tarot card and said that it showed I have inner strength and courage. She wanted me to know that Steph is not earth-bound - that she is "way up in heaven" with the mothers (her grandmothers) and is at peace. She said she is trying to get through to me and I told her I was trying too, but with no success. She said I am too close and my emotions are getting in the way. She suggested a meditation and said that imagination is the key.

Elizabeth saw poems and songs being written about Steph, and said that she touched a lot of people when she was here. I did write a poem about Stephanie and her stories are touching thousands of people through her father's hard work. She asked if we knew someone named Michael, (we did) and she said that Steph was helping him because he has 'been where she was'. She asked if we had planted flowers in the back of our house recently and I said I had, late this summer. She saw flowers and said Steph liked them. She saw Steph as very creative. Then she said Steph's funeral was 'massive' and there were beautiful music and flowers. That was absolutely true.

She said Steph is on the other side with two good friends and that since she died she has helped someone else cross over. She sees Steph there with a cat and a dog that wasn't her dog but was MY dog (Patti) when I was growing up. She drew another card and it was the moon looking down on two cats. We do have two cats, Toby and Buster. She said one of the cats was one Steph left behind (true!) but that it fights with another cat around the same time every day (true!). Stephanie had a very annoying cat that doesn't like anyone and fights with the other cat all the time. She said Steph sent love to her cat here.

She saw my mom sewing and I said that rang true, that she sewed a lot, and she said, 'Well, she's still sewing on the other side!' She heard the songs 'I Will Always Love You' from 'The Bodyguard', and 'Would You Know My Name if I Saw You in Heaven?' by Eric Clapton. I think of Stephanie when I hear those songs.

She said Steph was very feminine and was handing me a pink rose. She saw my Dad sitting in a favorite chair. Then she drew another card and said there is gold at the end of the rainbow and there is much happiness from the spirit world. The last thing she said was that I was wearing Steph's bracelet that day. I was. It was the only thing of hers I was wearing. I had run back into the house to put it on before I left! Anyway, it was all remarkable for its truth.

Stephanie at her Flagler High School Graduation

Young Stephanie, one of Terry's favorite pictures.

Opposite - More treasured pictures of
Stephanie with Mom & Dad.

~ Sydney ~

~ ~ ~

Joe was next. When Joe went in she told him he owned six properties and that his son's name was on some of the deeds (true). Joe asked her to tell him about his son.

She said, 'He's passed over.' She also told him that he was laughing at Joe for being so adamant about wanting his shoes!

When the third parent went in she told her that we were supposed to be together as our children are together in heaven. So, there it all is - our day in a nutshell.

That night I shared my story with everyone and all agreed it was remarkable. I have taken out my notes and I read them often. It has helped me a lot just knowing that Stephanie and all the young people are all there together and are happy. I pray all of it is true!

I found the reading very comforting and returned to see Elizabeth about a year later. I'd never spoken to her since and had spent only that one half hour with her the first visit. This visit the cats came through again. I told her I'd almost had to put the one to sleep he was so bad. She told me that would be fine with Stephanie; she would love to have him with her!

Life is difficult. We feel the pain and long to be released from it. How do we do that? Visiting Elizabeth was one of the things that truly helped.

&&&&*Reflections by Elizabeth* &&&&

* Stephanie and Sydney *

One day a while back, three people came for a reading. I was busy, as usual doing readings, so I just knew I had another three until I would be finished for the day. The first came in. It was a lady who had lost her daughter. Her daughter came through with a lot of information for her mom. I could feel the burden lift from her mom as her daughter gave her so much evidence. I always ask before I start a reading in my prayer, "Please God, send the highest healing for whomever comes in my little room for help."

Stephanie was the name of the beautiful young woman who came through for her mother. I knew she had other young souls with her waiting for their turn. I felt the excitement of the young energy all over the room. Stephanie's Mom, Valerie, and her husband had done so much good work for people who have lost their children through suicide.

Stephanie was so proud of her parents and so pleased with the good work they were doing. Her mom left the room with a lot to think about and mull over.

Then the next person came in. It was a gentleman and I asked for his first name. He told me his name was Joe. I felt a young man around him. What a handsome boy, I kept thinking. So many young people and this one, what a sense of humor!

His father was so devastated. I've seen grief, but I was worried this man might never get his life in any order. I felt he wanted so much to be with his son.

Sydney wanted to make sure his Dad didn't do anything to hurt himself! He wanted to convince his father he was okay so he would get on with his life, so the evidence poured out, things that only his father would have known.

He asked me about his son. His son came through very strongly and he had such a good sense of humor. He knew just what his father had been focusing on and he made us laugh.

His son told me his Dad had a new puppy that kept lifting its legs on the son's possessions his father had kept. Sydney wanted him to keep that puppy away from his stuff! Joe told me the puppy had just chewed up Sydney's shoes and we both laughed.

I met with Joe for a second time. The man who came into my room a year later was NOT the same man. He seemed robust and healthy; I could tell he'd been able to move forward in his life. He was very happy with his reading.

*When I asked Sydney if there was a message
about his suicide, he just said, "Don't, don't do it!"*

༈ ༈

Elizabeth is one of those rare people who come into your life and leave footprints on your soul. I lost a son in 2004 and never had the opportunity to tell him goodbye. I don't think we are ever ready to say goodbye to our loved ones, especially not a 22-year-old child. I needed to know where he was, and what he was doing. I needed for him to know how much his mama loved and missed him. When I had my reading with Elizabeth it was as if my son was sitting right next to me and we were having one of our wonderful chats. She talked in his language and his great sense of humor had both of us laughing. To say I am grateful for Elizabeth, and the wonderful gift with which Spirit has blessed her, is an understatement. Elizabeth helps heal our wounds, opens our hearts, and teaches us all that there are always...Heavenly Opportunities Positively Evolving...

Pattie Hall

~ DJ ~

Chapter 6

Darla and DJ

Darla is a beautiful woman who radiates strength of character, compassion and caring. She works as an Emergency Medical Technician, but, her greatest love and accomplishment is creating a warm, welcoming home for her family. The neighborhood children love to play at their home and the neighbors often drop by for a visit. Darla's life was changed forever on one tragic day. Darla shared her story of loss and her joy of finding hope through discovering proof that life continues after the death of the body.

Darla's story:

We were the all-American family. My husband Doug and I had a wonderful marriage of 16 years. We had a 14-year-old son, DJ, and a 12-year-old daughter, Carlee. On February 4, 2004, our whole world was shattered. DJ was riding his go-cart, which he had just gotten three days earlier. He was hit by a truck and killed instantly.

Doug happened on the accident scene

a minute later. I was at work. My nephew was sent to tell me and bring me home. We are all so devastated. DJ was such a wonderful kid. He was on the go 24/7. He was compassionate and caring for everyone. DJ was a hugger. He hugged everyone. If he liked you, you would know it because he would give one of his great hugs every time he saw you. I miss those hugs so much.

When you lose a child it is so different from losing other people. My father had died three years earlier. We were very close and I thought I would never be able to handle the pain of losing him. It was truly horrible, but nothing compared to losing DJ. Losing a child is a pain that doesn't cease.

I worried about him. Was he sad? Did he feel pain? Did he see the truck and feel terrified? Did he miss us? I had so many things I needed to know. The grief was eating me up. I was so worried about my boy. I'm still his mother and felt he should be home safe with his family.

One day I was in a baby re-sale shop, and I got into a conversation with the lady who runs the shop. Somehow we got on the subject of DJ and she asked me if I believed in psychics. I said, 'Oh yes. I would love to find one.'

She told me about Elizabeth and how she had gone for a reading and she told me that Elizabeth was right on the mark with everything. Inside I felt the first glimmer of hope in a long time, maybe this was real! She gave me Elizabeth's number and I immediately called from my cell phone, but, had to wait two months for an appointment.

My anticipation grew every day. Could Elizabeth be real? Would DJ be able to communicate with me? How would I know it was really DJ?

Finally, the day arrived. I took our daughter Carlee with me. I wasn't sure if she would be allowed in but she really wanted to be there. When we arrived Elizabeth said Carlee should probably wait outside. She didn't want to scare her, so Carlee went outside to wait in the car and Elizabeth and I went in the room to begin. Before I sat down, Elizabeth said, 'Your father has passed.'

I said 'What?'

She said, 'Your father has passed and he is here with you in a very strong way. You were very close to him and he's with you all of the time.'

Elizabeth went on to explain that my father had a brother, which is true, and that he was there with him. She also said my maternal grandmother was there and she was saying we had gotten very close before she died and that she was with me a lot. I've always known Grandma was around. Sometimes I can smell her perfume, and we had gotten very close before she died.

Elizabeth said, 'There's a young energy here.' I got excited, but I didn't say anything, I hoped against hope it was DJ. 'She's standing off away from the others. She is Catholic and she's holding rosary beads,' Elizabeth said. I was disappointed but knew she was talking about my sister-in-law who passed away from cancer in her early twenties.

I asked Elizabeth then if there was anyone else. Inside I was asking whether DJ was going to be able to give me a message? My heart was pounding inside my chest with anticipation and hope.

It must have been so loud Elizabeth could hear it, because she said, 'Be patient, there will be more.'

Your father is pointing to you and saying, 'That's my baby.' He keeps telling me that.

'Were you the baby of the family?'

I said, 'Yes, he always told everyone that I was his baby.' He had used those exact words when he talked about me to others.

Then Elizabeth said, 'There's another young energy coming ...a young spirit that has a lot of energy.' She said, 'Your father has his arm around his shoulder and he's saying that he is a very rambunctious boy, but he is taking good care of him.'

I began crying and I said, 'That's my son!'

She said, 'He misses you, but he's with his grandpa and they're having fun. He's showing me fishing poles. They went fishing here and they are fishing there, Elizabeth said.

It was true. DJ and his grandpa had loved to fish together! At least I knew Dad was there to take care of DJ. Then DJ was telling Elizabeth someone was wearing his shirts and sweatshirts, and if he were here, he would not let that happen.

I said, 'Yes, his sister is.' Elizabeth said, 'Then maybe it would be good to let Carlee come in.'

I agreed it would be good for her and went out to get her from the car. Carlee was excited to be invited to come in, and we explained to her that her Pappy and DJ were there.

Elizabeth told Carlee, 'DJ is saying you are wearing his shirts and sleeping with one of his shirts, and if he was here, he would kick your butt, but since he's not, it's okay!'

Carlee was wearing DJ's shirts and sleeping with one. DJ often used the phrase, 'I'm going to kick your butt,' when he and Carlee had a disagreement!

Elizabeth said, 'He died in an accident, but it wasn't a car, it was something small and square. He's saying it wasn't his entire fault. He couldn't stop and the man was going too fast.'

I asked if he felt any pain or fear when he was hit.

Elizabeth told me, 'He said no. It had all happened in a split second. He saw the truck, was hit, and passed over all in the blink of an eye.'

I asked if he misses us as much as we miss him.

Elizabeth said, 'He said yes, but he is helping other kids who have passed and they all sit and talk about their loved ones and it helps all of them.' He's talking about his buddy who is very talented musically.' (That was DJ's best friend, Cody. DJ always called him 'Buddy'.)

He mentioned his friend Danny. 'He

misses him a lot and says to tell him 'Hi.' He's also talking about Jim,' Elizabeth said.

DJ had a friend Danny we hadn't seen since the accident. When DJ was alive, our house was always filled with his friends. We had also been adopted by an elderly couple who lived near us when we moved from Ohio. They became our surrogate Grandma and Grandpa. DJ had been very close to Grandpa Jim.

Elizabeth also mentioned that I was sleeping with a bear every night since the accident as it reminds me so much of DJ. Carlee had been asking me if she could have the bear, but I'd told her she had DJ's shirts, so she should be content with those. How could Elizabeth have known abot the bear and the shirts, unless she was truly giving us messages from DJ?

The time I spent with Elizabeth was one of the best hours since losing DJ. I knew in my heart that he was right there, so did Carlee, and through Elizabeth we could once again have a conversation. It did so much for my soul and lifted Carlee's spirits. I could see it in her face and knew my face must look the same. There was so much specific information about me, Doug, Carlee and our lives before and since the accident that Elizabeth could never have known.

~ ~ ~

Postscript: On the drive home after the reading Darla and Carlee saw DJ's friend Danny for the first time in several months. They stopped to give him the message from DJ, which he was surprised and happy to receive. Darla gave Carlee DJ's old bear; it reminds her that DJ still loves her as she loves him. From the Reading with Elizabeth, Darla, Doug and Carlee found great comfort in knowing DJ is still a part of their lives.

~ Jason ~

Chapter 7

Patti and Jason

When Patti heard about Elizabeth she was on a waiting list to see George Anderson, the famous psychic medium written about in the book, We Don't Die.

It had been months since her son Jason was killed in an automobile accident and she was desperate to know if he was okay. There was a waiting list of over six months and she had already sent a check for $1,000 to secure her reading.

Patti said, "After my reading from Elizabeth, I called and got my check back, I wouldn't go to anyone else now. I got everything I needed from her reading!"

Patti's son, Jason, a beautiful, vibrant 22-year-old, loved life. Patti has a video of him skydiving on his 18th birthday and maneuvering his lean body under a burning pole, only inches above the ground. He was an expert at limbo. While working in the family business he loved to travel to the South Seas.

Jason was Patti's only son. At the time of the interview, Jason had died almost two years earlier when the car he was a passenger in hit a pole and flipped over. It had come to rest in his own front yard and Patti and her husband were there immediately after they heard the crash.

Jason's best friend was driving the car. He and his friend and two girls had been out late at a Daytona Beach club. According to the others in the car, Jason wanted to know just how fast the car would go. The two girls as well as the driver survived. Jason was the only one in the car who died. Patti learned about Elizabeth through some other parents who had lost their children tragically.

Patti's story:

I went to see Elizabeth in February 2003. I truly believe everybody needs to do two things in life: go to Disney World and go see Elizabeth! I learned about Elizabeth from some other people who were in a grief group I attended. I don't think Elizabeth realizes how valuable she is, how much she helps people! I don't know what I would have done.

After Jason died I was going in circles. My mother and my sister, who were both skeptics, went with me to see her. She blew everybody's mind. When my mother came out from her session with Elizabeth, she was just shaking. My sister went in first; because my mother wasn't sure she wanted to go in at all.

I said, 'That's okay, you don't have to go in if you don't want to.'

Then my sister came out, and while I was in with Elizabeth, she told my mother every thing that Elizabeth had said. After that my mother started to get a little excited, so when I came out, she went in.

My mother had been completely skeptical. She was 75 years old. When she came out she said, 'Oh, my gosh, Elizabeth told me things that even I had forgotten. I just sat there with my mouth wide open.'

She told my mother that it was her mother who was the first one to meet Jason on the other side. Elizabeth kept saying to my mother, 'There are Bibles all around him, Bibles, Bibles and more Bibles.' Elizabeth said, 'I've never seen anything like that. What is it with the Bibles?"

What Elizabeth didn't know was that every time there was an anniversary or special date, my mother would donate Gideon Bibles. After Jason's death I kept getting cards in the mail saying my mother had donated five Bibles in Jason's name. So, when Elizabeth did my mother's reading, the Bibles kept coming up.

Elizabeth said, 'There are Bibles and more Bibles and I don't know how they are connected to you, but I just keep seeing Bibles coming to you every couple of months.' Then Elizabeth said, 'He just loves the Bibles.'

Then Elizabeth told my mother, 'You are from a family of six children and you are the only one left here' (true). 'I see your mother in the kitchen cooking' (as she always was!) 'She's wearing an apron. Your mother wants me to tell you that she's up there cooking with her friend with a name that starts with an M.'

My mother couldn't think of who she could be referring to. She said, 'No, no...' Then Elizabeth said, 'You know him, you know him!' My mother said, 'Well, it's sure not Grampa!' Then Elizabeth said, 'He has trains all around him. He's surrounded by trains and he's Jewish.' Well, my mom all of a sudden knows who she's talking about. My mother said, 'Oh my gosh! You mean Moe!' To which Elizabeth replied, 'Yes, yes that's who it is.'

When my mother started telling my sister and me about this we said, 'Who is Moe?' We'd never heard of anyone named Moe. So what my mother told us was that when my Grandmother was young, she had a friend named Moe who worked at the train line. He would let Gramma Kramer go on the train to sell sandwiches and fruit. My sister and I had never heard that story before. We had no idea that our Grandmother used to sell food on the trains. My mother told us she had forgotten about it, but Elizabeth knew it. That was so awesome!

Elizabeth went on and on to tell my mother all kinds of things. That was something. We learned some history about our Grandmother from Elizabeth that had never been told because it had happened way back before my grandmother was married. I never knew that my Gramma Kramer was one of those girls who used to come on the train to sell food.

The night before I saw Elizabeth I was going through anxiety. It was just the unknown and I didn't know what to expect. I kept telling myself to get some rest. I was asking myself, 'What if he says this or what if he says that?' My mind was clicking and clicking. I was trying to predict things and I set myself up. None of the things I feared happened. Much more important things came through that day.

Once I saw Elizabeth, I felt really comfortable. I could feel the peace in her mannerisms, her personality. Nothing amazes her, and nothing shocks her. She keeps on a level that is very reassuring. When I went in and sat down Elizabeth said, 'Oh my goodness, there's a boy, a handsome young guy jumping all around you with beautiful eyes!' Elizabeth said, 'He's about to knock you off the chair.'

Right then, I was hoping my chair would just spill over! Then Elizabeth said, 'There are Js, Js, Js, all around you, all around...there are J's.' I thought, there are. My Dad's name is Jim, John was his buddy, and of course Jason! Elizabeth went on, 'Well there are J's all around you...the young man is so happy. He's jumping up and down.' Then she said, 'Your son's name was Jason!' Just like that. 'He's at peace on the other side.' Then she said, 'He has received a diploma on the other side and he graduated to the next level quickly.'

The funny thing is that the only other psychic I'd seen, in Cassadaga, Florida had told me the same thing.

Then Elizabeth told me, 'He wants you to look after yourself. He knows you have a great support system; that you are surrounded by good family and friends; and he wants you to continue writing in your journal. He is much respected on the other side.' Then she said he went very quickly and he didn't feel any pain at all.

~ Patti and Jason ~

She told me my maternal grandmother was there to greet him and that my grandmother now has a beautiful home in the countryside. Elizabeth told me, 'I can see that when your grandmother was here, her house was small and she lived in a very crowded city but now she has a beautiful countryside home.' It was so true because my grandmother Kramer used to clean for the church and they gave her a little house to live in. If you opened the window you could see the inside of the neighbor's house.

Elizabeth then said, 'I keep hearing Eric Clapton, Eric Clapton singing, 'Would You Know My Name, Would You Know My Name'. He keeps making reference to that song."

That was uncanny because at the time I was making Jason's video. I was trying to decide whether to put that song in. I love that song, but I was thinking, of course he'd know my name. Because of Elizabeth's reference to it, I used the song. That settled the matter.

Next, Elizabeth said, 'You have a piece of jewelry you wear close to your heart that represents him.' That's true, it's my necklace. My nephew made it for me for Mother's Day. It has his picture in it and on the back it says, 'always in your heart'. That blew my mind too. Elizabeth told me, 'I see music, videos, and writing in a journal. This whole thing started out small, but, it's getting bigger and bigger.'

Boy was that true, I thought it was going to take seven days and it ended up taking seven months! I started making the video in February and it wasn't finished until September. That was the video of Jason that I was working on at that time.

Then she told me, 'He is concerned about someone like a grandfather figure.' That would be my dad. Elizabeth said, 'He's playing tricks on him to get his attention and his grandfather thinks he's going crazy.' I said, 'What kind of tricks?' She said, 'Doorbells ringing, telephones ringing, you'll find out when you talk to him.' I did find out. Jason was doing that.

That night when I got home, I called my parents to read them my notes. My Dad was on one

103

line and my Mom was on the other. I said, 'He's playing tricks on you like ringing the doorbell, turning the lights off and on...'

My mom said, 'What about the telephone?' Almost daily the phone was ringing, and there would be no dial tone and the line would be dead. Then, once a week, the doorbell would ring and Dad would go to the door and there would be nobody there! Dad had gone out and changed the doorbell, and it still rang. He wanted to disconnect it and my mom wouldn't let him. She told him 'No! Don't disconnect it. I like it.' He said, 'Well it's driving me crazy!' My Dad was 100% skeptical and now he's only 80%. Now, when the doorbell rings, my Mom will go to answer it and if there's nobody there she says, 'Hi Jason'.

And then the tree! Oh that was something. Elizabeth told me, 'He wants you to stop worrying about the tree.' I have to tell you this briefly. I had planted a tree for Jason the first August. It was for his birthday. I planted this little tree right in my driveway area and this tree wasn't making it. It kept getting brown and limp and I kept putting fertilizer on it and giving it a lot of energy. I was going on the Internet, researching it, and I could never get it to grow. I never told anybody but every time I would pull into the driveway I would get so upset. I kept thinking, 'What is wrong with this tree?' I felt so bad!

'Well,' Elizabeth said, 'I don't know what this means but he's telling me to stop worrying about the stupid tree! If it doesn't get any better, just get another one.' Well, I said, 'Oh thank you.' I've been working on this tree for so many

months. I came home and ripped the tree out of the ground. Before that I would have felt guilty. Now, Jason was letting me know I needed to stop worrying about it!

Elizabeth told me, 'He really enjoyed playing cards while he was here,' which he did, and she said, 'He's still playing cards with an old gentleman in the spirit world.'

She said, 'He also wants you to go ahead and get the curtains you've been thinking about.' I still haven't gotten the curtains, but, I knew the ones he was referring to! She told me a lot of other stuff as well. For example she said there were four people in our house, and a new person who needed to be there because he'd been through a lot. That was true. She said someone was getting a new computer...that was my husband.

Elizabeth said I still had some of Jason's clothes and that I sleep in his T-shirts. True! Elizabeth said, 'When you wear his T-shirt, it is Jason wrapping his arms around you. He likes that. Keep praying because every time you say a prayer you are throwing up blessings to him and he can feel the vibration.'

Then Elizabeth said, 'Jason had a very strong relationship with your mother. I can see her slipping him money.' She always did that, not just to Jason, but to all the grandchildren. She would always slip him five dollars or something and tell him to go get something to eat. She thought nobody knew it.

She also told me about the accident. Elizabeth said, 'I see the car. It hit a pole. There were people coming from all around. There were three other people besides him; they were fine (true). It was just not their time to go. Your sister could not do any more for him. He was already gone before she got there. He was looking down watching. You had a premonition immediately when you heard the accident that he was gone.' That was true, I did have a premonition, and my sister had tried to save him, but it was too late.

Elizabeth told me, 'He's doing a good job on the other side; he's working with young people. You must understand that the world is very, very small in the big picture. He enjoyed playing football, and he loved it very much. I'm not sure if he's still playing football or soccer. He's playing cards and football. He's filled with a lot of young energy. He has divine guidance.'

Then Elizabeth said, 'He's telling me you have a dog who is with you now. He's laughing, because he says you have the new dog, and he's got the old dog.' My old dog, Buster, who died before Jason, was as good as gold. My new dog Max, who was Jason's dog is very goofy and is driving me crazy. Elizabeth said, 'He's laughing because he said the new dog drives you crazy!'

Max is very aware of Jason's presence. I believe Jason comes around the dog a lot and the dog knows it. My nephew and I are often in the living room with Max. All of a sudden Max will start looking at something; he'll start looking all around. If we call him, he pays no attention to us. About four months ago, the TV in my bedroom started just turning off...at no special time of day, not daily, just every once in a while, it would just turn off. Then all of a sudden it would come back on. Max is always in the bedroom with me and when I turn the TV off he just lies there, but when the TV turns off by itself, it's different. He jumps right up. When it comes back on, he'll lie down again as if nothing happened.

Elizabeth said Jason told her, 'Don't look back, just let everything go.' She also said, 'He's very surprised at his face! He says he looked very good at the funeral.' What he meant by that was the fact that we were worried about how he would look at the funeral because of the accident. He was right, he did look good. She said, 'He's really very funny. He has a great sense of humor!' That would be Jason!

Elizabeth went on, 'I know that he wasn't cremated. Did he have an open casket? I keep seeing cremated. I keep seeing cremated, cremation and a casket.' At that time, I was thinking, 'Who do I know who was cremated? How do I put this together?' Elizabeth said, 'It will come to you.' It did later!

There was a message for a friend of mine too. Elizabeth wanted to know, 'Who is the Italian friend who loves to cook?' I told her that would be Mary Grace. She said, 'Tell her that her mother says hello.' Then she told me, 'Jason wants you to remember all the good things. He knows you have love, love, and more love for him. He knows there's a memorial coming up and you'll be getting a lot of ideas for this memorial. You will renew friendships with people you have not seen in a while...who is Craig?' 'Craig?' I asked, 'Could that be my sister, her last name is Craig?' She said 'Yes, he is acknowledging her.'

Then she said, 'Someone lost a baby (true)

and he is helping the baby.' There was a stillborn baby.

Elizabeth said, 'Do not analyze things too deeply.' Then she would go onto something else. She said, 'I see things changing in your house, moving furniture around or remodeling.' I was doing both.

Then she came back to the cremation. Elizabeth said, 'There's that cremation again. I keep getting cremation and the casket.' I still didn't have any idea what that was about.

Elizabeth told me, 'Remember always that the worst thing that could ever happen to you has already happened. It can only get better. You are strong, very strong...' Then she would go on to something completely different. 'He said he enjoys his studies. He is VERY handsome.' I loved that. He really was a great looking kid.

Elizabeth told me, 'I see jean, jean, and blue jeans. This might sound weird, but do you have only one pair of jeans?" I said, "Oh my goodness Elizabeth." On the way over there I was with my mother and my sister. We stopped to get gas. I got out to pump the gas and they went over to smoke a cigarette. When I went over to get them, they said, 'Are you losing weight?' I said, 'I think so. I have only one pair of jeans that still fits me.' He was even at the gas station with us! Do you believe that? 'Nobody has just one pair of jeans.' Elizabeth said, 'He says he wants you to get more jeans.'

Then Elizabeth told me, 'There goes that casket and cremation again.' I still didn't have a clue but she just kept on going, 'He likes that big picture of him, the one you had blown up.' I have the picture above the mantle and it was when Jason was a little boy. He's holding Buster the dog he said was with him in heaven. Then Elizabeth said, 'You have made a religious commitment recently. You have a broken heart that will never heal, but, if you continue to pray and be strong it will get better.' That was it for my reading.

Next my mother went in to get her reading and when my mother came out a half hour later she was just beside herself. She was literally shaking. My mother said, 'Patti, Patti, Elizabeth wants me to tell you something. The cremation...it is Jason's brown dog, Buster, and they are together all the time.' It hadn't even hit me that Buster, the brown dog next to Jason in the picture on the mantle, died eight months before Jason and we had him cremated. His urn was on the mantle and we said whoever went first, thinking it would be my husband or me, would take the urn along. We ended up putting it in Jason's casket. Elizabeth picked that up. She kept saying 'I see cremation and the casket,' and, when I didn't pick up on it, Jason came through for my mother and said, 'Tell her it's the brown dog!'

This experience not only had an impact on my mother; it also opened my mind as well. I used to be closed-minded about this stuff. Now, I know what death is - I can feel Jason all the time. I can't even say as some do that I'd give anything to have him back. I can't say that. It's not time for him to be back. I understand that now.

I forgot to mention that when I left the house Elizabeth gave me a hug. She said, 'This is from Jason; now go buy yourself some jeans.' It was truly awesome.

I've gone to Elizabeth many times to take other people, but I've never had another reading, I didn't need one! I just loved going to Elizabeth and everyone I've taken has received the same kind of consolation. They too have felt reconnected to their loved ones. I know now that he's not really gone which would be so sad. Of course I really miss him, but, thanks to Elizabeth, I now know that spirit is much more powerful than the physical.

Jason and John, about 7 or 8 years old,
both danced in a Hawaiian show.

John, Jason's best friend, tells his story:

We were heading back home and I was speeding and lost control. We hit a telephone pole and the car rolled over three times. Jason and the girl flew out the window from the back seat. When the car came to a stop I had to get out and go find them, they were lying across the street. Jason died on impact. Right after that I didn't really care about living. I was pretty suicidal for a while. Elizabeth gave me comfort. She told me Jason knew it wasn't my fault; it was his time to go. She helped me deal with a lot of stress. It's kind of like when you go to see Elizabeth it takes a lot of weight off your shoulders because she can really tell you a lot of things that you can't explain to yourself. It's made me not afraid of death.

Jason and his friend, Junior, in Tahiti

ᥱᥱᥱᥱᥱ *Reflections by Elizabeth* ᥱᥱᥱᥱ

* *Jason ~ Pennies from Heaven* *

Beautiful Jason. What a nice young man. Jason was 22 years old when he passed to the other side. It was nearly two years after his death that his mother Patti came to see me. Jason was able to give his mother an abundance of evidence through my reading with her. Patti was so warm, but around her I could feel an exuberant energy.

The energy of Jason was vibrant before and after his death. He had lived without fear, from skydiving to fishing. His death took a terrible toll on his family. His friends came to see me yesterday. He immediately came through for them. One of the young men was driving the car that Jason was in when he died. Jason told him to get on with his life. He said to tell him he wished him well and was able to share with him through me some of the latest news. He let him know that he still knows about the changes going on in his life. Just like all of these young souls who seem to be connected, and know each other in the spirit world, Jason is now on a mission: a mission of love.

On the afternoon I gave this reading I found pennies all over the sidewalk. I understand that Jason brings his mom pennies, pennies from heaven.

ᥱᥱᥱᥱᥱᥱᥱᥱᥱᥱᥱᥱᥱᥱᥱᥱ

Elizabeth,

I wanted to let you know how much you mean to me. My sweet child died in a car crash in December 2005, and I know this. I am not looking for closure. What I have found in Elizabeth is an affirmation that his spirit lives and that he continues to be a vibrant force. My sadness is forever and all consuming, but when I see Elizabeth, I feel the presence and love of my son very strongly and my sadness is more peaceful. From my association with Elizabeth, I have come to realize that my son is fine, he is just in a different place - my visits to Elizabeth are now for me. My son is my life and will continue to be. He knows that I will always be sad because he is not physically with me so he visits with me and Elizabeth, and, through her, he imparts some wonderful piece of wisdom that I keep in my heart. Thank you, Elizabeth.

Judith

❧A Historical Perspective ❧

The Spiritualism of Grace Cooke
Notes taken from: *Minesta's Vision*

Grace Cooke was a gifted medium in England during her adult life. Her gift is something that was with her since childhood. After the death of her mother when Grace was seven, her family had become interested in the Spiritualist movement taking place in England at the time. From that age it became normal for Grace to see the spirits of those who had died and to hear their conversations. White Eagle, an American Indian guide had visited her from a young age. He most often came at night or would be waiting when she woke. Often he came alone but sometimes he would bring Indian spirit children or other people he wanted her to know. He would bring children of every race. Grace would play with these children.

When Grace was twelve a member of her family took her to visit a neighbor who was a complete stranger to her. The woman was extremely ill. Grace looked off into a distance in a trance-like stare and saw a little girl holding a doll. The little girl said her name was Lilian and she asked Grace to tell the woman who was ill that she would not die as she thought she would and that she would return to South Africa.

Then in Grace's vision the scene changed and she saw a beautiful veranda and a man smoking a corn cob pipe.

"What's wrong Grace?" she was asked by those in the room who noticed her stare.

"There's a little girl here, and she wants me to tell

you something," Grace replied.

The woman started to sob. The little girl was her daughter. She had died three years earlier. The man on the veranda was the woman's husband who was in South Africa. The little girl Grace spoke to wanted to show her mother the doll to let her know how normal life was beyond this life and how well and happy she continued to be. Grace was filled with 'joy and happiness' at being able to give this message of hope to Lilian's mother. The woman had believed she was dying and was resigned to her fate. She didn't die when she thought she would and was able to return home to her husband in South Africa. Grace's prediction was fillfilled in less than five months.

Grace Cooke spent her life serving people through her trance readings. Grace Cooke's work is now a part of the international White Eagle Lodge which publishes the beautiful messages to bring comfort to the grieving.

❧ PART II ❧

Elizabeth Palin

Elizabeth's First Communion

Elizabeth Age 13

Elizabeth in Liverpool sitting for a portrait.
Opposite - 19 years old, partying with friends.

Elizabeth and Husband Harry

Opposite: Elizabeth, Harry and daughters
Simone and Denise.

Elizabeth and granddaughter Jessica.

Opposite: Elizabeth and Harry on vacation.

Elizabeth and Jessica

Elizabeth in her home in Celebration, Florida

~ Elizabeth ~

Chapter 8

Conversations with Elizabeth

When I met Elizabeth Palin that winter day in 2002, I was struck by the beautiful redhead that answered my knock. Almost instantly we became friends. I was fascinated and appreciative, but I also wanted to understand how she was able to do what she does. I continued to want proof it was real. I began to spend time with her and with people who received readings from her. I interviewed people whom I knew she had no way of knowing anything about. I was like a detective on a search for truth. Elizabeth helped me so much personally in solidifying my beliefs about death and life after death.

After getting to know each other we soon realized how much our work had in common. We both strive to bring comfort to the grieving; I, as a bereavement counselor; Elizabeth, as a gifted intuitive able to act as an intermediary for the deceased and their living loved ones. We each held an important key that could help people in the midst of their emotional pain. Several months after first meeting, I sat with Elizabeth and she began to tell me her story.

Elizabeth is just plain fun to be with and her personal story is fascinating. The more I learned the more impressed I was with her extraordinary skills and her wisdom. There were so many things I wanted to know. We had numerous conversations and during them I had the opportunity to ask her many questions about her life growing up in Liverpool. We talked about her years in England, her recovery from alcoholism, her intuition and how it began to open up, and she answered questions about what she has learned over the years.

The first thing I asked her was to elaborate on her life in Liverpool. Elizabeth's autobiographical story is now being recorded in another book that will be released in 2007, but the following is a brief overview. I'm sure this interview will be as intriguing for you as it was for me.

L. Shannon Andersen

~ INTERVIEW WITH ELIZABETH ~

Question:
Elizabeth, would you mind telling me about your childhood?

Elizabeth:
I was born in Liverpool, England and was raised Catholic. My Catholicism was a big part of who I was. The people in my community were poor. Life was hard. There was a pub on every corner of Scotland Road where I lived. Scotland Road was the dividing line between the Catholic and the Protestant. The Catholics were on the dock side and Protestants up the brew. We all lived in tenements with our families in close proximity. Our elders wouldn't allow us to mix with each other. 'Scotty Road' was known for its liveliness and for good humor. I think that's where I got my sense of humor. They say you need a good sense of humor to live in Liverpool. The people were warm and friendly. They were good neighbors and they pulled together during the war. They pulled together at other times as well.

By the time I was nine months old I had lost my mother to tuberculosis. I also lost two uncles in the war. I had a lot of losses early. My father was a bosun's mate in the Merchant Navy and he was at sea when I was born. His work kept him away for months at a time, so when my Mum died, I was raised by her mother, my

Grandmother 'Lizzy' for whom I was named. My older brother Alexander and I lived with her on Burlington Street off Portland Gardens. It was just off Scotland Road in the tough, inner city.

Your mother died and two uncles died as well. You grew up with a lot of death.

I did. I always knew I had angels and I was never afraid of death. It was so common that the women of the community were the ones to help prepare the dead. My grandmother did that as well. She would prepare their bodies for the wakes. In those days there were always people dying, young and old. I was a Catholic, I had been taught the souls of those who passed over had to be prayed out of the flames of purgatory, so when I was a little girl I would kneel at the coffins of the people who were 'laid out' in the community. I would say three 'Hail Mary's,' three 'Our Fathers,' and three 'Eternal Rests,' in the hopes of helping their souls into heaven. I took it very seriously.

I'd spend the entire All Soul's Day in prayer trying to get as many souls out of purgatory as possible. I found great satisfaction in believing that those people I prayed for were out of the flames through my prayers. When I was nine, I used to go alone into St. Anthony's Church and read the letters left on the altar by all those who were asking St. Anthony's help. Then I would light the candles and say a prayer for them. I never had the money to pay; still I would light the prayer candles anyway. I often left the entire altar ablaze. It was a wonder I never got caught, but I wanted to make sure St. Anthony heard the people's prayers.

My father stayed away at sea until I was fifteen. Even though he was away a lot, I loved my father very much. He was a hard man, full of swearing, and a face that was well lived in. He was born in August, as I was, and he loved to dance and to drink as I did. He had lived ten years in NYC before I was born. He drove a cab there in the 1920's. At one point he ran a dance hall. As I remember it, he used to dance like Fred Astaire. I loved dancing with my father. I never had a good relationship with my stepmother whom he married not long after my mother died.

It sounds as though you were close to your Grandmother.

I loved my grandmother very much. She was a good-living woman who prayed for everyone and everything. Her consolation was going to mass and benediction. That's where she found peace. My Aunt Martha, her daughter, was a spinster. She worked in Edmondson's Sweet Factory, so when I used to walk with my Grandma she always let me walk with my hand in her pocket and there was always a chocolate. Martha used to get an allowance of reject sweets once a month. I always loved that time of the month when we could have a chocolate!

With your father away, living without your mother, it sounds as if you must have had to grow up very fast.

I did. I started drinking when I was a teenager and alcohol nearly claimed my life before it was over. Luckily though, years later, I realized I was an alcoholic and got into recovery, but Liverpool in the 60's was an

exciting time. Paul McCartney, John Lennon, George Harrison, and Ringo Star were all on the scene. I knew the members of Jerry and the Pace Makers. Liverpool wasn't that big, and in those days, the Beatles and many of the bands hadn't made it yet. We hung out at the Cavern, The Blue Angel, the Temple and all the other clubs. It was a time of caps, mini skirts, and boots and I looked good in them!

I can remember Margot's coffee shop. The Beatles would get kicked out for acting foolish. At that time I was living a double life. I had a daughter by then. I was Mum by day, but by night I partied in all the clubs with mates my own age. My sister would baby-sit for me. I would pull an overcoat over my mini skirt and a scarf over my head to catch the bus at 10:00 in the evening. The coat and scarf would come off as I stepped into another world of dancing, music and friends. I'd stay out at the clubs until three or four in the morning and then catch the bus home in time to get up and go to work the next day.

I worked at Dorothy Perkins and then at Moss Brothers Department store in the Bridal Department. With the money I earned, eventually I was able to buy a car, an Austin 35. I smashed that one night right in front of the police. Even though I'd been drinking, they let me go and I caught the bus home. It took a long time before I finally hit bottom with alcohol.

When I'd go out, I'd have one cigarette in the pack and 10 bob in my purse. All I'd have to do is order my first drink and that was the last one I had to pay for. I used to hang out with two beautiful girls, Maureen and Diane. They were so much fun. We'd do 'the bunk' on the guys. By that I mean, after they bought us a drink, we'd disappear into the ladies' room and then go out the back door to another club. It was all done in fun for a laugh.

My family was very proud of my working in the posh department store. They were poor but they were very proud. Once, Auntie Martha and Auntie Mary came to town carrying their patchwork bags for the loaves of bread they were going to bring home. They wanted to see where I worked, but did not want to embarrass me. It was not typical for people from the inner city to go into such a posh shop. They had no business there. When the manager saw these two old ladies carrying their bags, slinking along looking very suspicious, he thought they were probably shoplifters.

He came to me and said, "Look out for those two peculiar looking characters peeking around the corner. You better keep your eye on them!"

I looked over embarrassed to see my Aunt Mary and my Aunt Martha. They were looking very suspicious because they didn't want to get me in trouble and people from the inner city just didn't go in shops like Moss Brothers! It was very posh from my blessed aunts' thinking. For my manager to think they were potential thieves couldn't be further from the truth!

When I told my father about it later he said, "That boss of yours didn't know he had Mary Magdalene and Our Lady right there in his midst!" He really had a laugh over that one.

It sounds as though you had a lot of fun.

I did. I was typically shy, but when I was drinking I would do anything. I was the life of the party and could be very entertaining. I used the alcohol to overcome my insecurity and it made me crazy. In those days alcohol became my friend, but it got me into all kinds of trouble, including causing fights. Everywhere I went I caused mayhem. There were so many times when I was drunk and did really stupid things, crashing cars, insulting people. It just continued to get worse and worse. I was becoming a big problem drinker, but had no idea. It certainly wasn't all fun.

Things changed in my life when my father got cancer. He became very ill and was in the hospital at Christmas. They allowed the patients to come home for the holiday. My first husband, father of my daughter Denise, and I were not getting along. He was away at sea all the time and never home. I wanted to get a divorce. My dad moved in with me at Christmas and survived for only 9 months. During that time I realized just how terrible my marriage was. Dad helped me get the courage to divorce. The marriage was dysfunctional from the start. It was very co-dependant. The divorce was the best thing that could have happened. My father supported me and gave me the courage to go through with it. He died the day after the divorce was final. It was as if his job was done. Thus began another chapter of what now seems like a soap opera!

What happened after your father died?

I continued to drink and my drinking continued to worsen. I worked in a club called Toad Hall and in the Aughton Chase Riding School where I tended bar. I was trying to support my daughter on my own, working at three clubs at once. I would drink in the evening and sleep while my daughter was at school. I also worked in an electrical shop part-time during the day, trying to save money. I was taking pills to stay awake so I could be home for my daughter Denise by 4:00 in the afternoon.

It was about that time that I met Harry, my second husband. He was a big cuddly bear. He had a nice house, a big car, and he drank a lot. At the time it seemed perfect. Harry also had a really big heart and in actuality he saved us. We were friends before we started going out and finally, we moved in together and married. Harry had a little girl, Simone, and once again, a light came into my life when I adopted Simone.

The common love of alcohol seemed to make Harry and me a match made in heaven. We would drink every night, and go to the clubs. We continued to live the party scene. I kept on working but only part-time. I was able to spend time at home with the girls. Unfortunately, my drinking got worse. Because of Harry we had the money to maintain that lifestyle. We lived in a massive home on the beach. It belonged to Harry's father and when Harry's father remarried he asked us to leave. We moved into our own home and the drinking accelerated. I wanted to party every night.

Those were really crazy times. I remember ending up in a nightclub one night with bedroom slippers on. We'd have terrible fights. I was starting to get paranoid. It was a vicious cycle. In the morning I used to get up and pull myself together but when Harry got home, we'd start the drinking again.

It was my daughter Denise who started to tell me, "Mum, you need help." She was right. When they talk about reaching bottom in Alcoholics Anonymous, for me that would have to be the night the family now refers to as 'The Last Supper'.

Was it at this point you realized you had a drinking problem?

Not really. I was still in denial and Harry never saw it. He never realized that the alcohol was killing us, or at least me! The evenings would start off being nice and by the end of it we would almost kill each other, at least verbally. Even today Harry says, "You've never been an alcoholic. You just couldn't take it." I know different. I was on automatic, in an alcohol created fog. I just couldn't think.

Then, the night we called 'The Last Supper'. That was the last time I ever took a drink. In the week leading up to that night, I drank every day. I was nasty, horrible to everyone in fact. I had beer before I came home and the hard stuff at night. We were going to a big social event, a wedding in a Marquee, and we were accompanied by my youngest daughter, Simone, and a friend. It was very dressy and I was drinking malt whiskey and champagne. The alcohol in my system was like a boil ready to burst. At the event that night I wreaked havoc on the whole place. I pushed the singer off the stage. I threw my high heel and hit a famous football player in the head. I went into a black out. I couldn't remember anything until I found myself trying to crawl through a doggy hole trying to leave as the room was in chaos.

It was then that I collapsed.

All of a sudden all I could see was my body on the floor. I looked like a pathetic heap. I was above my body looking down and there was a woman beating on my chest. I was dying before my own eyes. I didn't see angels, or heralds or white lights, but I knew I was dying. When I realized what was happening, I knew I had to go back. I could feel Harry shaking me. He and our friend carried me out of the wedding. Simone and her friend Linda were both crying.

When I got home I woke up and was still falling all over the place. Denise called the police because she thought Harry had pushed me when we were getting out of the car, but he hadn't really. When the police came they told her, "Your mum needs serious help." I lay in bed for a week and I began to detox.

It was horrible. I had the "DT's". I was shivering and vomiting. Harry sent Denise to the pharmacist who gave her something for me to take. I was hallucinating. I thought people were trying to murder me. It was Denise who saved my life. She said, "Mum will you go to AA? Please Mum, you are very ill and you don't know it."

It was Denise who helped you break through the denial then?

Yes it was, but it didn't last long. I told Denise I'd go to AA, but at first I wasn't serious. I decided I'd pretend to go and then I might find myself a good man to get me away from all the craziness. I had no intention of listening while I was at the meetings. I called a man

and his wife who were members of AA.

"My daughter made me call," I told him. He asked me what my symptoms were and when I told him, he said I should drink sweet drinks. He said in a few days he and his wife would come around to pick me up and take me to a meeting. I told him, "I'm not an alcoholic." He told me I didn't have to be an alcoholic to go, but that I should attend the meeting anyway. I asked him the color of his car and a few days later I dressed up in a chic outfit and waited outside for him and his wife to pick me up. Ken and his wife became my saviors. They took me to a meeting twice a week. He was like the father I'd lost. His wife was in ALANON. They practically adopted me. I am still so appreciative of them for all they did to help me in my recovery.

The first week I stopped drinking I looked ten years younger. I've never looked back and I've never had a drink since. For the whole first year I never spoke at a meeting, I just listened. I didn't say I was an alcoholic for two years. I watched and listened. It was like being a voyeur on my own life. I was judgmental and critical, and unforgiving of myself. I continued to attend AA regularly. I also began other work on myself. I went on to complete the EST training (a workshop for personal growth) along with other personal growth work.

Seventeen months after I joined AA, I started volunteering with hospice and I began to help out in the AA meetings. I became treasurer. I was a terrible treasurer as I would accidentally spend the money and have to figure out how much I'd spent and put it back.

After two years, I began to speak at the AA meetings and became a group leader. It was the EST training and personal growth that really helped me with the speaking. When I finally spoke, I said I was an alcoholic and it was then that I really started to do my recovery work. That was when my intuition began to open up.

It was at AA that you began to become psychic?

Yes, I started to sense things. I began to see auras around people in the AA meeting, and I could see things like a brandy glass in their hand. I knew what they drank when they were drinking. Gradually people began to notice my skills and people were drawn to me for healing ability. I started to do a lot of my healing work in my own way. My psychic ability started to develop. It was very strong, but the thing is it didn't happen until after I started to serve others and not be so self-centered.

Did you have any teachers who helped you?

Loads, but one in particular. I met a woman named Miriam who had been the leader of the Southport Spiritualist Church. She became my mentor. It was with her that I started to sit in 'rescue circles'. Her house was a house of healing. Every Wednesday afternoon and Thursday evening she would have a group at her home. Those of us in the group were taught to send out healing to people who were sick and to places of strife on the planet. My experience with AA began to lead me to new levels of learning. I learned about the ancient wisdom and the Cabala; and my intuition continued to improve through the practice in Miriam's circle. She was a medium and she nurtured me and helped me learn to do what I do now. Miriam used to say, "You can do it. Don't be scared. You've got it there. Open up and let them use you." I will always be grateful for Miriam and for my experience with AA.

It was while sitting in AA meetings when I started to pick up the passed-over ones. At first it scared me. It seemed as if they were sticking to me, but gradually my gift developed into a tool so I could use my ability to help heal others.

How long have you been in America?

I moved to the United States in 2001 and I never intended to keep working, but the word got out. Now, my calendar is solidly booked months in advance. I even do readings in France, Spain, and England as well as most of the U.S. and Canada. I can do readings even on the telephone. The funny thing is that, when I was a teenager, I went to a psychic in Liverpool with my girlfriend. The psychic told me I would become very well known and would one day go to live in America. I walked away saying, "Now I know this is a load of rubbish." Nobody went to live in America at that time from where I lived and me, I hadn't been out of Liverpool. In 2003 while living in a suburb of Orlando, Florida, I was approached to do a television pilot and other people are writing my biography. Here it is, all those years later and it seems I'm living out that prediction.

Elizabeth, I have been so impressed by your talent to act as an intermediary between the living and their loved ones who have passed over, as well as your extraordinary intuition about the past and the future; but, I have to say your life story is very interesting as well. I admire your willingness to share your recovery from alcoholism and your work with AA. I too grew up in the 60's, I am most impressed that you actually knew the Beatles! Do you mind if I ask you about them? Do you remember when you first met any of them?

No, not really. Liverpool was a small community. I didn't have to be introduced to them. We all went to the same clubs. We were in the same group of friends. We were just friends. When I knew them, they weren't playing in the clubs; they were just hanging out at the clubs. We would go to the same coffee bars. Everybody had a guitar in those days.

There were a lot of groups that came from Liverpool. I just knew the Beatles as nice boys. One of them married Maureen who was one of my good friends. She used to live off Scotland Road and she was lovely. She married Ringo. Another one of my friends was married to Les McGuire who played the piano in Jerry and the Pace Makers. We all knew the Beatles were different. After they went to Germany, they really made it. The Beatles were just one of the groups in Liverpool, but, of course, as everyone knows, they had a different style about them. I just knew them as the lads. Half of Liverpool knew them. Everyone was happy that they made it as they put Liverpool on the map.

A lot of people had Liverpool slated as a tough seaport. There were a lot of artists and creative people who lived there. At the time there was so much

going on in Liverpool. It was an incredible place to be in the 60's.

Where did the people of Liverpool originally come from?

Liverpool was a natural 'pool' where the old sailing ships tied up in the Mersey Estuary and it served as port and natural shelter. The port increased in size, largely because of the slave trade to America but mostly with the advent of the Industrial Revolution. Lots of trade meant lots of work, so many people came from Ireland, Scotland and Wales to fill the jobs. The combination of these people helped develop our exceedingly rare accent which didn't exist prior to the 19th century. Before that, everyone had the same accent as the rest of Lancashire. Most of the people from my neighborhood were from Ireland. They were hardworking people with common sense and survival skills. Scotland Road is famous really for all the people who lived there. All of them were characters. There have been a lot of movies, stories, songs, and sea shanties written about Scotland Road.

I believe you said you remember hearing the bombs during the war. Is that correct?

Yes, I was just a little child but I remember VE day. We all had a party in the streets. We ate jelly (Jell-O) and custards. That was a nice memory. A lot of the kids from Liverpool got evacuated to Wales, but my brother and I didn't. I can remember being handed out the window in order to get me to the air raid shelters when the bombs were being dropped. We would stay in the shelters until the air raid was over. We used

to live in a block of tenement houses. On the next block of tenements, one street up, a bomb hit one of the shelters and everyone was killed. A priest used to come to bless it. There was a lot of death and poverty in those times. We had a stew called Blind Scouse. It was made of bones and a few potatoes, maybe a carrot. Because of that, we were often called Scousers.

Those were poor days, and there was so much death. People used to put blinds down when someone died. They would hang white sheets in the windows. When they did, we would go to show our respects. The body would be laid out for three days and neighbors would come. When I was very little, I used to go to kneel down and say a prayer for the dead. Lots of young people died too. There were horses and carts and lots of children would get run over. Many of the women lost babies as well. There was always someone dying of diphtheria or pneumonia.

You grew up in a time where you were surrounded by death. Did you always know that death is not the end?

Oh yes, I don't know if it was because of the Catholic background, but, I think that gave me a very good grounding for what I tune into. I've always believed in the Holy Spirit, and the Virgin Mary appearing to everybody. I believed in miracles. I always loved my guardian angel. Without him I never would have gotten through my childhood. That, however, is another story on its own.

When was the first time you remember consciously communicating with spirits?

I don't know, consciously I don't remember. I know that I've always spoken to my mother who passed over. I also know I've always had guardian angels and that I've always spoken to them as well.

Do you envision your guardian angels?

I used to, but I don't have to anymore. For years I did, but now I just know they are with me. I've had the same guides and angels for years and years.

Do you remember when you told me about seeing your mother when you were sitting in a spiritualist circle?

Oh yes, that was so, so real. That experience was the most vivid experience I've ever had. I had my eyes closed but I could see her. It wasn't scary. She was so loving and she was calling me and saying, "Come to me, you know who I am." I've never felt so much love in all my life. It was warm and beautiful. I was taken aback at the time. There was a part of me that blamed her for leaving me when she died. I was just a baby when she died.

The group sitting in the spiritualist circle helped me to bring her through. It was a rescue circle, and I used to give all the messages. I would tell which spirits were there and what kind of help they needed. It was a rescue circle for the earthbound spirits. Everyone in the circle would join in and talk to the spirits to help them move on.

It was a real shock when my mother came to me. The entire group could feel the incredible love that was all around. I was amazed. I was shocked. For

years I hadn't thought of my mother. It was Miriam who watched the circle to make sure everyone was okay. She's the one who helped me to realize that I hadn't forgiven my mother for leaving me. I realized it was true. It was so hard growing up without my mother. When that happened, I was able to release those feelings of being abandoned by my mother. That experience was another step that helped me start doing what I do now.

Elizabeth, if I am correct, I believe you've said that the key to your intuition is your imagination. Is that true?

That's right. The key to psychic ability is your imagination. You should never think that you are imagining anything because you have to ask yourself, "Where is it coming from?" Imagination and intuition come from the same place, your subconscious mind. Without your imagination you can't reach any level of expanded consciousness. You have to open up to your imagination. Our imagination has been deadened over the years, so I encourage people to use exercises for their imagination by reading fairy tales, or doing other things that will fire their imagination, like reading poetry. I also suggest they just start sitting still and letting their imagination take them. What I am suggesting is daydreaming or meditating. Just giving your mind some space to see what comes, and then just look at it. Imagination and intuition are definitely linked.

Do you mean we should watch the pictures that come in the mind?

Yes. If you want to contact a loved one, you can go to

meet them using their imagination. It is like taking an active role in creating. I tell them to go to a beautiful place in their imagination, a garden, or a beach, anywhere they would like to be. Then find a lake or a body of water and make a stone path to follow seven to twelve steps and have it lead to another lake where there might be a bench. When you get to the bench just see who is waiting. During the process you may think, "Oh, I'm just making that up," but that's the way the spirit world can get to you...by opening up to that level of consciousness.

Elizabeth, are you saying we can all do psychic readings by tuning into our imaginations?

Oh yes, you can do the same thing a medium does for you; you can learn to do for yourself. You just have to start somewhere. You know a lot of people aren't aware of their own psychic ability and that's why they go to mediums; they don't realize they can do it themselves. It's like learning the piano; if you keep at it you'll learn it.

It sounds as though you just have to have the courage to tune in and say what you are experiencing. Is that the message you are trying to share with people? Are you saying you just go with what is coming into your imagination?

Yes, and you know sometimes you get the most stupid things but if you just start saying it, the people you are reading will know what you are talking about. Whatever comes to your mind. It might be a symbol or a metaphor. I used to use the tarot cards for divination, but I don't really use cards much anymore. It's just

something I used to keep my focus. As for the spirit world, I can sense the spirit world. Sometimes I feel them, and sometimes I'll see, or feel the energy. I always know when it's a young energy because the energies go so fast. They get really excited. Can you imagine being in the spirit world and having a chance to say hello to your mum? They get so excited and they talk so fast it's hard to understand them. I have to say, "hang on, hang on." Sometimes it gets overwhelming because I can feel the energy pushing and trying to get there, talking fast. Sometimes it's hard to concentrate and pick it up.

A lot of the people you've done readings for say that you start mimicking the hand motions that their loved ones would use, like stroking their hair, or you might use their slang.

It takes a lot of energy for them to come through. You can't just switch it on. It really takes a lot of energy from them and from me.

Elizabeth, tell me about your coming to live in America.

If you remember, I told you earlier about the old psychic on Queens Drive I went to see with two of my friends when I was 16. She looked at me and said, "YOU are going to end up in America. You are going to live and die there and you are going to be very happy." I thought to myself, America? I have never traveled anywhere. The only place I'd been at the time was to New Brighton on the ferry across the Mersey. Then I was sure it was a lot of bunk! She went on to say, "You are going to do very well, when you go to live in America."

For years I did my work in England. First, I learned the tarot. I was taught by a few people, but, eventually I started to do it my own way. As I said, I used the tarot as a point of focus. It was a way of opening up to my ability. The ability to do readings continued to open up over time. I just had to learn to trust it. I always had it. I just needed to learn to trust and know that I was being guided. I needed to learn that I was just an instrument.

I had self-doubt for years. I always knew I could do it but I didn't have courage. I felt as though people would think I was crazy. I practiced for years, long before I started doing readings for a living. I had to realize it was not coming from me. It was coming from the Source (God). After I had my Near-Death-Experience I knew I had to go back into my body and to serve for the rest of my life. I knew there were things that had to be done because it wasn't my time to go. There were no angels, no heralds; I just had a knowing and a feeling. It was after I got well that I realized how bad I had been. I didn't think I would never ever drink again, but I haven't.

That's quite amazing.

It was not easy because there were people drinking around me all the time. I never thought I would give up drinking for life. I thought I'd get well and then go back to it. It never happened that way. I just went further and further into developing my intuition and it was as though I removed a big block in my intuition when I quit drinking. I opened up to a new level of consciousness. I was quite excited about what my path was going to be.

I knew I had to do a lot of work and it would take time, but on the path to doing this I did a lot of volunteer work for hospice. I used to talk to the patients about death and heaven and I would tell them my experience. I used to watch the people as they were dying. Sometimes they wouldn't let go. I could see their loved ones were waiting for them but they worried about 'who's going to make his dinner,' or 'who's going to be there for the kids?' I'd tell them the kids were all grown up and they could manage without them. I would tell them to look for the light and look for the people waiting for them. I'd tell them what had happened to other people and to me so they could let go. So, often they didn't want to let go.

There was one woman who was really, really ready to let go. They sent for her daughter from Australia and she came rushing in, so the woman kept hanging on. The daughter would beg her, "Please don't go," the woman was suffering terribly. "Please, I need you." I could see she was hanging on for all the wrong reasons and I said to the daughter, "You don't understand about death. It's only a transformation and you need to let her go to a better place. She will always be in your heart." The trouble is, we get selfish and we want them in the flesh. People need to understand that in the transition they are much better off.

I don't think we are ever really ready to let go of our loved ones.

We are all going to die and someone is going to lose us one day. We are all going to lose loved ones, but, isn't it better to know that we can still have contact, to know there is a spirit world and that there is a life after death? Do you know something? We really never know anything. All I know is that twice I nearly died; once when I was drinking and another time when I went to have an operation. When I came out of surgery, I started hemorrhaging and I found myself out of my body, looking down. I thought, "That woman is dying." Then I realized it was I who was dying. I could see all the doctors and the nurses rushing around.

At the time, all I could think about was my loved ones. I just wanted to let them know I was okay. That was the very first thing I thought. I really thought I was dying. That Near-Death Experience happened about a year before the other one. It didn't change my life like the one that followed. With the first one, my daughters flashed into my mind and I knew it wasn't my time. I've been in a lot of car accidents and I've been thrown out of cars and lived. There has to be a reason for me to be living and serving.

Elizabeth, in many of your readings you talk about animals being with their owners. Is that often the case?

Oh yes. That's the case. I quite often see that people and their pets are together and people can look forward to meeting up with their pets again. Their spirits go on to their lot on the other side as well. What I've been shown is that there are people who look after them as well. If there are no loved ones over there, there is always someone looking after them. There are always other spirits that love animals waiting for them. There is an animal kingdom as well. So again, there is a spirit world and a spirit world for animals.

Pets get to be with their owners?   Are you saying people can expect to see their beloved pets again and animals get to be with their families as well?

Yes. I see that all the time.

You've talked about your volunteer work with hospice in England. Can you tell me a little more?

Yes. It was a time when I was coming to terms with death myself. I'd been through a lot. I had been quite ill and I'd nearly died so I used to go to hospice and do massage. I had done a massage course and I had done Louise Hay's workshops so I spent about two years going to the hospice about three times a week after work. I would go to people who didn't have any visitors. I'd just talk to them and give them love and healing and peace. It was an experience that really made me feel humble.

Did you talk to them about death and dying?

Not all the time. I was there to support them mentally and emotionally as well. I used to send them good thoughts. If I could speak to them about it I would, depending on the patients. That was really a nice way to volunteer. It used to give me a lot of peace. A lot of people who knew they were dying were interested in the spirit world and their loved ones and I used to talk to them about that, if they were open to it; only if they were open to it.

I was talking to a nurse the other day who came to me for a reading. She said she could see the fear on so

many people's faces before they make their passing. She can see their struggling and then she said she can see them giving in and she sees that calm that comes over them. She says it's absolutely amazing to see that. Well that's how they tell me it is when they are passing over. When I started the hospice work I was starting to go into the spirit world more than anything else. I wanted to use this gift that I have in a positive way. That's why I did the deep communication courses, the EST training, and another called 60 Hours of Being a Human Being; and then I volunteered to help others. I've done all kinds of things to make myself strong in preparation for my work.

Elizabeth, in many of your readings you talk about life on the other side going on as if it were here. You talk about people having homes and jobs and getting diplomas. Is that the case?

The spirit world recreates what they would have liked here. For example, they can have the house they always wanted. In readings, often I will describe a house and people will say, "Oh that's the house they always wanted or that they always envisioned." That's what happens in the spirit world. In the spirit world we can create anything we want. It's a mind world. They can create anything at all. They can be what they want to be. Sometimes they come to me as a younger spirit. Sometimes they are with a husband who passed away years ago. They come as a couple and they show me their best memory. It's a world of mind.

Is that a state that is temporary? People don't remain in that state for eternity, do they?

Yes, it's just a state, a stage, and then they eventually move on to the next stage. When they evolve, they go on to the Halls of Learning where they learn about the tools of reincarnation. At that time they get to choose if they want to come back and do it again, or if they want to stay and learn more, and come back later in another lifetime.

Do I understand you to say we are able to create mentally all the things that we love? What you are describing sounds a lot like the heaven we are told about. Is that what it is? Then, as I understand it, we move on, and begin to learn more. Eventually, we get to decide what we want to do next?

Yes, you move on, and some souls stay in that stage and help with the souls coming over. Sometimes I'll say, "You know your son's still here and he's helping other people, because that's the state he's in." It's just like it is here. Eventually he'll move on. We learn here and then we move on…well, Heaven's the same.

I've noticed in the readings you've done for parents of young people who have passed over that you've said they were now working with children and animals.

Yes, that's right, like attracts like. When young people die, they can understand the grief other young people are going through. They know how difficult it is for them to leave their parents and friends behind. They can help because they are children themselves. They work with children for as long as they need to. At some point they'll move on and begin to learn more themselves about how they are evolving. There's plenty of time for that.

I would think the young people who have passed over want more than anything to let their parents know they are okay. You have a gift that helps them to communicate with their parents. You've demonstrated that gift over and over again, giving specifics, names and details from their lives that only they and their parents might know…but I am also sure, as you have said, that their parents can learn to use their own intuition to tune in to their children. Do you have any advice for those who want to improve that ability to communicate and feel their children closer?

Well a lot of times when you've lost a child, or other loved one, the emotions are so strong, sometimes it blocks them from really being able to communicate with their loved ones. Emotions can be like a fog around them and that can keep the spirit world from coming through. It is because of their grief and the pain. Their loved ones are there and waiting. Sometimes they can come through via a medium. There comes a time when they start to move on. I think it's a good idea to learn meditation, to be quiet and just tune-in. The spirit world is a world of the mind and when the mind becomes quiet, they can begin to visit. I suggest they start by using their imagination and bringing their loved ones to mind. That opens a door for them to come through. They can read books on meditation, read how to sit still and tune in and within their quiet minds ask them how they are doing, then listen to their thoughts, hear their voices, and just see what happens.

You are saying they should just bring a picture of their loved ones to their mind?

Then ask them for help, or ask for some evidence that they are okay and then just sink into it. Given the chance, those on the other side will do their utmost to get through. It may be when you open a book and find in the words or in a phrase something you've been looking for, or you may find a sign that only you would recognize. When you get a sign you'll just have a knowing on the inside and you should always say thank you. All you have to do is ask.

Never ask them to come back because they don't want to. They are in a better life; and if it is possible rejoice in that fact. Often people need to have proof to survive the pain of grief but I say try not to pull them back too often. It's not a good thing because some people can get stuck in their grief. Our loved ones on the other side are on their own soul path over there to help and serve. Grief and pain and wanting them back here all the time might hold them back. They need to go on eventually and the happier you are the easier it is for them to let you go as well and move on.

Just talk to them as you would talk to them here. You can ask, "How are you?" You can tell them what is going on. They already know anyway. I tell people if they start getting an inner vision, they need to trust it.

Are you saying if they feel their loved ones near, they should just go ahead and talk to them?

Don't treat them any differently from the way you would if they were alive. It's really the same as when they were here. Tell them off if you need to. I remember a friend whose husband died and left her with six little

children; and every Sunday she would take them to the graveyard. She would line them all up and would say, "Now Alphie, this one has done this, and that one has done that…" You know it worked. In the end she was communicating with her husband. In the beginning she thought she was making it up and then it moved to another level and he actually helped her raise the children. He remained very much a parent in the lives of the children.

You're saying it feels as though you are making it up until it becomes real to you?

Yes, because where do you think it's coming from? That's the only way they can get through, via your thoughts and the pictures in your mind. Theirs is a mind world.

Did it feel that way for you at first Elizabeth?

Yes, that's exactly how it felt.

Sometimes when you are doing a reading, it is as if you are seeing the person standing there. Some people say they can see you looking over their shoulders at someone. Is that true?

Well, sometimes I do see. Sometimes I see a silhouette, sometimes I truly see. Each time it is different. It is rarely the same.

Then some come through stronger than others?

It depends on the link really. Sometimes my energy is low. Sometime I can see only a silhouette or hear a

voice but sometimes when the energy is high, they come through clearer. It depends on me and…it depends on the spirit world as well. It also depends upon the beliefs of the people who are sitting in front of me. There are people who put up a wall and just won't let me in. It really depends on many things.

Is it kind of like tuning a radio?

Yes it's like a radio. It's like turning a radio on and trying to find a station, sometimes it's really clear; sometimes it's really fuzzy. Sometimes I can't catch it because it's really fast. The world of spirit has a faster vibration than the vibration in this world.

You learned to do what you do gradually and over the years. It isn't something that just came to you.

No, when I was a child I was always different. When I say different, I have always had the gift of communication. The time that this really came to me was when I got very ill and nearly died. It was, as I mentioned earlier, my Near-Death Experience. That really launched my search. After that I began to explore. After years of working on my intuition I knew I could do it but I didn't know how. I was like all others interested in tuning in to their intuition. I had the skill available but, I didn't know exactly how to tune in. I learned how to do it. If I can do it…so can everyone else.

All people have the ability to the same degree. I seem to have the ability that comes naturally. It's just like any other talent. So, I can tune in a little bit differently.

Everyone can do the tuning, and keep working with it until they get it right.

It was after your Near-Death Experience your intuition opened up. How did this actually become a business for you in England?

I told the story earlier about my Near-Death Experience (NDE). It was because I drank too much. I was at very low ebb in my life. I had everything, yet I had nothing. I had a big hole in my soul and I didn't know what to do about it. So, I used to drink quite a bit. I had the big house and the family. I didn't know where I was going. The drinking became a problem and I got sick and had the NDE. After that I stopped drinking. I started to go on a program of recovery, and I started to open up. Then I began to sit in a spiritualist circle. I began opening to my intuition. The others could see that I had the ability. I could never see it. It took me a long time to begin to realize I had the ability!

Even for you, as talented as you are, in the beginning it felt as if you were making it up? Then you are just listening to the thoughts that come into your head and the images that come to your mind?

Yes that is right. I am just saying what comes into my head, what I'm seeing in my imagination; and it turns out to be true. I am still getting convinced, even now. Eventually, I gave up worrying about what I was saying because now I know it is connected to my Source. It's taken me years to convince myself. So now I just say it. I've given up worrying about it

When did you actually make this your career? I know you

had a very big business in England, a huge following of people. It became so big you were running from it when you came here because you were so busy and you had hoped to slow down. How did that happen?

I used to work every day until six or seven. I would work from nine in the morning until seven at night. How did that happen? I don't know. People just came, people who needed help.

Gradually, people suggested that you start to charge for your services? How long ago did that happen?

It just sort of happened. The people just began to come and my home became a healing center. People would come to sit in my garden. It became a garden of peace and before I knew it I was seeing people all day long. It just took off. I started to do the Tarot because it gave me a tool to do what I do anyway. I was a bit nervous sitting there, telling people about their loved ones at first. Not everyone wants to hear from their loved ones. So I did the Tarot as well.

You never really wanted to be a medium did you?

No, I never, never wanted it. They tried and tried to get me to stand in the Spiritualist Church, but, I never wanted to be in the spotlight and that was the honest truth. I've never wanted to be a medium but I knew I had the ability and everyone else knew it. It was that ability that drew people to me.

You've never been able to avoid it.

No, I've been forced by those upstairs.

Is that because it is your mission?

Yes, and it is a mission. I've never, ever wanted it, because I am so light-hearted. I thought it would be really heavy, but it's not you know. It gives the people on the other side what they want and helps others here as well.

You found yourself so busy in England that, in the end, you finally decided it was time to leave. Didn't you tell me it was after you found someone lottery numbers?

No, not exactly. Two ladies came to see me and they were very, very rough, from the inner city. I told one woman something I never say to anyone, because I've had people say they had a psychic tell them they were coming into money and then they've gone out and spent all their money and gone into debt. Anyway these two women came and I said to this one, "You know you are going to be coming into a lot of money." She said, "Oh go on…what are you talking about?" and she left. As she was leaving she brushed by me and nearly knocked me off the chair. I said to myself, "I am not going to do this again." That was on a Friday and on Saturday she won the roll over lottery! Well, then I had all of her friends calling me! I knew then it was time to get out of England. I had been so busy for so many years, I felt burnt out from all the readings. My daughters had been asking me to come to America for five years, so I decided to come. I packed up and came over.

You moved to Orlando, Florida. When you came, you had no intention of doing the readings here. Is that right?

No, I was going to spend some time with my grand-daughter and maybe help my daughter with her decorating.

Now your phone never stops ringing.

I know. It's back again. It took only three months.

After three months here you started to do your work again?

It just came. I didn't open up for business, or look for business. Actually, I met a young woman. Two years earlier her mum had died. I sat next to her in the park when I was there playing with my granddaughter. I sensed her sadness and I said, "Have you lost your mum?" and I told her a few things about her mum. She said, "Thank you for that." I told her I was visiting my daughter. Three months after I moved here, there was a knock on my door and there she was. She said she wanted to thank me again and asked if I was doing any readings. I said no. She asked me if I would come to a women's club card meeting and do some readings. I agreed. She put me in a room and one after the other came in. I could hear the excitement rising in the room outside the door as they got their readings. After that all the neighbors started to come and that was that. That kicked me off, just word of mouth.

I understand you now have your own production company.

Yes, that is in the works. We've created some DVDs and videos. I actually created a system where people can learn how to read the Tarot themselves on their

computer or TV. It's really fun. I'm also working on a book about my life.

That's great. We are really lucky to have you in Orlando. You've told me some very interesting stories about how people found you. One was the story about a woman who was told by another psychic to go to "the woman with the yellow card." Could you tell that one?

That's true, that story! A lady rang me up on the telephone. When I was working in England you had to book six to nine months in advance, sometimes longer than that and people would never forget their appointments because they were too hard to get. They knew that if they missed they would have to wait a long time. In Fornsby where I lived, a lady rang me up and said she had an appointment. She asked if I could fit another person in? I said no, I couldn't, I had back-to-back appointments. I didn't have any time available. She begged, and so I said the best I could do was to give 15 minutes each, no more. She said that would be better than nothing. I forgot all about it.

When she came I started with the reading. After the first 10 minutes, I could feel the spirit world come around. I told her, "There's a young girl from the spirit world and she is about 16 and she has long blonde hair. I think her name is Lisa and she wants to talk, but I have the feeling she's not here for you." The woman said, "No, it's not me."

She rushed out and let the other woman come in. When she did I said, "Is this your daughter that I have here?" She said "Yes." And I asked, "Did she have Leukemia?" She said, "Yes." I said, "She's showing

me that in your bag you've got a photograph. There's one that you've got to rip up. She said she hates that photograph and it's getting you depressed. You were going to kill yourself the other night. But it's not that bad." I said "You've got to pull it out and rip it up right now!" She pulled it out. It was a picture of her daughter. She was all pale and with no hair and she was in the hospital. I made her tear it up.

I said "You've got another photograph with her lovely hair. That one you've got to keep, that's her now. That's the way she's showing herself to me now." Anyway I told her a few more things about her daughter.

When I was done I said, "By the way, how did you get my name?" I wanted to know, because she was from the south of England, outside London, which was a long way away. She said she had been to a big meeting of a well-known medium, and there were hundreds of people there. At the meeting he picked her out and said, "You've got a message from someone who has passed over to the other side, it's a young spirit. You are going north and you've got to see the woman with a yellow card."

That night she got on the phone to her sister and her sister asked, "How'd you get on at the meeting, did you get a message?" The mother of the young girl said, "It was stupid. He said I was going to see a lady with a yellow card, who would have a message for me." Her sister said, "Lord Almighty, the yellow card is here by the telephone, I'm going to see Elizabeth with the yellow card tomorrow!" That's how she found me.

When she left, I got on my knees and thanked almighty God that he'd brought her to me. I knew I might have saved her life. I said, "Thank you, God, for giving me some signs that give me the courage to go forward and do my work."

Elizabeth you often hear messages through songs, is that right?

Yes that's right. Sometimes I'll hear music. The song will run through my head. Sometimes it's when I'm talking about the funeral or if their Mum has just heard it on the radio. Sometimes the lyrics might have a message.

Your clients often have their own messages don't they? What are some of the most common?

They often see dragonflies and butterflies, geckos, lizards or frogs. Sometimes they get pennies, dimes or even quarters. They have told me about orbs in their pictures, birds, cardinals, eagles, or hawks. Quite often they see rainbows at important times. They get loads of different signs. They can also get other things like smile faces for one. It's just their children letting them know they are okay.

It seems the children somehow bring their parents to you. That's the reason I'm sitting here today, because one young man died and brought us all to you.

Sometimes I need to hear that. It's rewarding. It's like giving me a box of chocolates.

You also once told me about a lady who called you on the

phone for an appointment and you ended up giving her a message that might have saved her life as well.

Yes, sometimes it will come over me when I'm not expecting it, but that's not very often. One time that happened. This woman called me and it was late at night and I thought, who the heck is that? This woman said, "Is that Elizabeth?" As soon as she spoke, I felt this young spirit behind me and I felt my hair standing up and I felt his energy. I knew it was a boy and I said, "I don't want you to talk to me I just want to tell you something. I said I feel a young spirit around me and I hope you don't mind me saying this, but have you lost your son?" She said, "Oh my God." I said, "because he's here with me, and he's awfully concerned about you."

You've got to stop doing what you are thinking about doing. I can see the tablets and the whiskey and I can see you're thinking about killing yourself, and he doesn't want you there, it's not your time. Please don't do it, because you are really upsetting this young man." She said, "I've got the pills in front of me now and someone gave me your card a few weeks ago and I was about to do it when I saw your card in the fruit bowl. I thought No I won't call; she's like the rest of them. Then I thought, before I take the tablets, I'll give it a try.'"

Then I told her some other things about the accident. I said, "You've been trying to keep your spirits up. You were out at a party tonight and you were dancing and trying to look as though you were okay but your heart was in two." I said, "You have been drinking and trying to take tablets because you don't want to

live. He was your baby wasn't he?" Then I said, "Was his name Tony?" She broke down. She said, "I've got the tablets here and I was getting ready to do myself in. I can't believe it, Luv, you have saved my life." You know she brought loads of people to me and she started to come to me more often and I was able to tell her other things about her son and it gave her a reason to go on.

There have been a couple of people who have been on that brink of suicide. One came to me the other week and I told her that her son was hanging his artwork in heaven. She said her son was an artist and he'd died eight years ago.

If you were going to give advice to grieving parents what would it be?

I don't know. It is so hard. I would just hope that they could believe as much as I do that their children are okay and I would hope that they look for signs. That could help ease their pain. I'd say, "Just hang on." A lot of them may start feeling as though they want to commit suicide but that's not what the children want for them. They just have to hang in there and know their children want them to be happy.

I think people just want to know that their children are well and happy. I remember one parent who had lost his son. He came to one of your groups. His wife made him go. She had come to you after their son died. Her husband was skeptical but he came to your group and you led them through a meditation where they brought their loved ones to them in their minds. In his imagination he had seen his son standing before him with his hat in his hand down by his side. He watched him run his fingers through his hair and then put the cap on. When you began the group you went straight to him and began to talk about the young spirit who was around him. Then you described him running his fingers through his hair and putting the cap on his head. It was an incredible experience for everyone in the group that day, particularly the father. The experience began to give him hope that in some way, his son was okay. It also illustrates how intuition comes through imagination.

Yes, I do that meditation so they can learn that they can tune in themselves and it is through their imagination that they will come.

❧A Historical Perspective ❧

The Spiritualism of: Edgar Cayce
Notes taken from *Edgar Cayce: An American Prophet*
written by Sidney D. Kirkpatrick

Like Grace Cooke, Edgar Cayce's gifts were noted early in his childhood. Edgar Cayce adored his grandfather Tom. He would sleep wrapped in his overcoat or nestle up next to him his beard clutched in his little hand. Tom taught Edgar to ride and fish and would help him build forts in the wood. One day when Edgar was four he was riding behind his Grandfather in the saddle. He felt safe and content as his grandfather's drawling stories poured out as they took their regular ride. His grandfather told him tales of burning farms, of the War Between the States. He told him the stories his grandfather had told him, of Indian raids and battles in the west, of wagon trains and trapping beavers in the woods.

On this day's ride Tom Cayce let Edgar off to catch minnows while he watered the horse. It was thought that the steed was perhaps frightened by a moccasin which came out from under a log. The horse charged across the water and tried to jump a fence. Failing to make the jump, he reared and threw Tom into the stream; his hooves came down on his chest. Tom drown.

After the funeral Edgar was heard talking to his grandfather. His parents told no one about it but when Edgar went to live with his aunt Lou, she asked Edgar why he spent so much time in the tobacco barn. He explained that he was visiting his grandfather. He told her that "grandpa came to the barn to help the farmhands hang the tobacco." He only talked to Edgar, not the field hands, he explained to his aunt. He said he saw his grandpa working alongside them, helping without their knowing by reminding them of chores that needed to be done.

Edgar told his Aunt Lou that Grampa could sometimes be difficult to see, but that he appeared in "beams of light" that came through the rafters in the ceiling, and that he could often see right through him. Edgar wanted to show his aunt Grampa's favorite place to sit near where the robins had built a nest but she declined.

When Edgar could tell his aunt some of Grandpa's old stories Aunt Lou became very distressed. Unlike Grace Cooke who had the support of her Spiritualist family, Edgar Cayce's fundamentalist Christian roots caused his gifts to be viewed with fear. Edgar Cayce himself always viewed the psychic skills that developed in his life as a gift from God. He told his family, "If ever anything I say (while in trance) hurts one person, I will never do another reading." He worked up until his death serving people with medical, and spiritual issues. The transcripts of his readings, research and stories of his life and his work are recorded in volumes and housed in Virginia Beach, Virginia at the Association of Research and Enlightenment (A.R.E).

❧ PART III ❧

Recognizing the Signs
After-Death Communications

L. Shannon Andersen

Chapter 9

After-Death Communications

During the years I spent around this group of grieving parents, I heard many incredible stories; stories of personal "After-Death Communications" (ADC's). These ADC's were signs that came directly to many of the same parents who had found their way to Elizabeth. Elizabeth's readings were able to verify for those left behind some of their own signs and messages. Here are just a few of the stories.

Windy :

When I first came back into the house after Jody's death, I could smell him. It was such a strong scent. It was as if he had just walked by. I also felt him touch me; there were many strange things like that. There was a banging on the windows and when I checked, there would be nobody there.

Once, I went to the crash site with a girlfriend and she had a cell phone. We were trying to figure out exactly what had happened at the crash. While we were there, a 911 call came through at the sheriff's office from my friend's cell phone. There was no explanation. Her cell phone logs all her calls. We told the 911 Operator we hadn't called, and there was no outgoing call logged on the phone. We had not made the call. It didn't show up on her phone but, the really strange thing was the call came through at exactly the time the accident took place!

Christmas was only a short time after Jody's death. We had gone to Elizabeth and received some incredible messages but on Christmas Eve, Carol, Jody's mother, had gone to the site of the accident. The emotional pain at the time was excruciating for all of us. At the site Carol had told Jody, 'I need to see with my own eyes! Windy really needs that!'

Then at Christmas we all were just miserable. My stepfather wasn't there and Jody wasn't there. We were trying to be as upbeat as possible for my son. My mom and I took some digital pictures of the family opening presents. After things calmed down, my mother went into the computer to print them. I heard her say, 'Oh my gosh, come in and look.' In the picture there were two distinct faces, one was Bill, my stepfather, and the other was Jody. It was an answer to a prayer Carol had made the night before.

It was the next morning my mom and I took the pictures. We couldn't believe our eyes! We just stared at the picture and then we started to cry. I couldn't wait to show Carol. Jody had done exactly what she had asked; he had given us something we could see with our own eyes. They were both there. There was so much proof. I think it just requires opening your eyes and feeling their presence.

This entire experience has absolutely opened my eyes in so many ways. I think that happens whenever you come so close to death. I almost died. After the accident, before I gained consciousness, I saw my life going before me like a black and white flicker show. That is life transforming in and of itself, as was finding Elizabeth. We've taken so many non-believers to Elizabeth and she's been able to help a multitude of people. She certainly helped me. When I first called Jody's mother she said, 'Are you out of your mind?' She went with me, and then she took her whole family. They all received so much information and help. God put people such as Elizabeth on this earth for a reason and I understand that.

I had so many questions I needed to have answered 'by Jody'. Through Elizabeth he answered many of those questions. Jody also came to many of us with a reoccurring symbol, the smile face. For months, it showed up everywhere! We had just left a small bar prior to the accident. Incredibly, a few months after the accident, the bar changed ownership. Its new name was 'Smiles!' On the window they had painted a giant smile face. When I walked in there for the first time, the song I heard answered a question that was in my heart and head. I heard REO Speed Wagon singing, 'When I said that I loved you, I meant I would love you forever'. Jody comes through for me all the time in so many incredible ways.

~ ~ ~

Stacy (as told to the author):

Stacy has had so many signs from Shannon and her loved ones they deserve to be an entire book. I've charged Stacy with that task. I told her Shannon wants her to do it! She was a "star;" a pink star, to be exact, and I think she wants to be just that - a star - of her own story.

As I mentioned, one of the ways Shannon showed up for Stacy was as a pink star. On one particular birthday, Stacy told me she asked all of her loved ones to give her a sign. The first thing she saw when she went into her bathroom was a nickel, a sign from her "Aunt Pickle".

The second sign came when MacKenzie, Shannon's younger sister, spontaneously asked Stacy to draw a heart and write "I love you" on a napkin for her lunch box. This was a first; she'd never asked anything like that before. Next she said, "Write XOXO on it." XOXO was Stacy's sign from Janet, Stacy's sister.

At the bus stop Stacy saw a full rainbow in a cloudless sky! At lunch at Cracker Barrel one stranger pointed out a dragonfly, and another showed her a purse with ladybugs. Dragonflies had been a reoccurring sign, and ladybugs were a sign from Denise a good friend who had died young. By the end of the day she was still waiting for a special sign from Shannon.

She sat down at MacKenzie's desk to record all of the signs she had received throughout the day. She had never sat at MacKenzie's desk before or since, she later reported to me. After finishing the task, she looked up, and right in front of her, on MacKenzie's bulletin board, was a pink star, her sign of Shannon!

Pete, her husband, had incredible dragonfly stories including the day his own mother died. Pete had been going to mass every day since Shannon's death, and on that day there was a dragonfly inside the church that began circling him. He wondered if Shannon was sending some kind of special message.

When he got home he learned that his own mother had died (obviously to be welcomed by Shannon on the other side.)

The most recent sign Stacy told me about came in a drawing from a 7-year-old child they help support in India. His birthday is on May 13th, the same day as Shannon's. He sent them a Christmas card and on the card there were two bells and a pink star! The only thing he had ever drawn for them before were flowers.

I have to say I too have felt very connected to Shannon since her death. She has come to me in a variety of ways. On one occasion I had been trying to call Stacy all day long because I had dreamt of Shannon the night before and I wanted to tell her about the dream. I could never get past a busy signal. I was driving my car later that day on I-95 when a car passed me. The license plate said May 13, Shannon's birthday! I knew immediately I would get through if I called, which I did.

I often see 9:23 on the clock, the date of Shannon's accident and pink stars appear in my life as well. The most incredible story was about a year after Shannon died.

I was cleaning out a closet in my kitchen and I found some undeveloped film. I put it on the counter and decided to throw it away instead of developing it as I thought it was some insignificant pictures. My daughter Melissa came into the room and asked me about the film. She insisted on taking it to have it developed at the 1-hour photo.

When she returned she said, "You better be glad I developed that film. It had pictures of Shannon on it." I opened the pack and saw the most beautiful picture of Shannon. She was propped up in a bed looking like a princess. Behind her was hung a sheet that had been used by the kids for graffiti.

I called Stacy; "Can you meet me? I have something I want to give you." She met me immediately.

When I handed her the picture I said, "I have a feeling there is something significant written on the sheet behind her." When I got home there was a phone message from Stacy. "You were right about the message. Right behind Shannon's head is written the number 23, the day she died."

In the final stages of finishing this book I saw Stacy. She told me an astonishing story about Shannon. We had all received messages from the children through Elizabeth, and felt their presence in many other ways, but this story brought a new dimension to their existence on the other side.

Stacy told me about a young woman, 19 years old, who had won the scholarship set up at the high school in memory of Shannon. She had never met Shannon, but had often seen her picture and helped clean the bench placed at the high school in her honor. This young girl also knew Shannon's good friend Shawna who had named her baby after Shannon.

This scholarship winner was involved in a serious car accident. As the crow flies, it was only miles from where Shannon died. The young woman was driving down the long dark road and for some reason lost control of her car. It was 2:00 a.m., and there was no one around. She was knocked unconscious by a collision with a tree.

While unconscious, Shannon came to her. She assured the young woman that she was going to be all right and said she was going to get help. An off-duty police officer - for some reason - decided to take a drive in the middle of the night. It was he who found the car and got the young woman safely to the hospital where she was in fact "all right." When she awoke she immediately wanted to speak to Shawna. When Shawna got to the hospital, she told her that Shannon had come to her and given her reassurance that she would get help. She then told Shawna Shannon had a message for HER!

Shannon had told her to tell Shawna, "STOP worrying about me, I am okay!"

I was covered in chills and Stacy and I both cried as she told the story. What a beautiful reminder that the children are still with us and on another mission! It had been five years since the accident that took Shannon's life.

~ ~ ~

Leona:

I've had so many messages from Randall myself. Right after Randy's death, we took off to try to get away from it. It was horrible. I kept saying I wished I could have a sign that Randy was okay. I just needed something, anything to let me know. At the campground when I was sitting at the picnic table, all of a sudden I saw these drag- onflies. I had never seen so many! One dragonfly ended up landing on the table and it just sat there and looked at me. All that night, the dragonflies hovered around the camper. I told myself it had to be Randy and all the others that had passed. They were there letting us know they were with us. We've had many dragonfly messages over the years.

My daughter, Monique, had an incredible experience too. She actually saw a flash of light that she felt was Randall. A couple of weeks later, at Randy's memorial, she said she saw it again, but this time it showed up on a picture! The pictures taken that day, the day of Randy's memorial, were full of orbs, mostly purple orbs but there was one incredible picture of a rainbow colored orb right over my head when I was releasing two white doves for Randy.

Another thing is the dimes. I had a friend who told me a story about her father and dimes. He had read a story in the paper about ''pennies from heaven,' and he told her, 'If I die I'm not leaving pennies, I'm leaving dimes.' The day Randall died, all my friends were here and this one friend called to ask how I was doing. She said, 'I asked Pop if Randy was with him and I no sooner said it than I found a dime.'

She explained the whole story to me and said, 'That's probably going to be your sign too, so look out for the dimes. You'll know that Randy is around when you find the dimes.'

It was amazing, because I got off the phone with her and went outside. I found my first dime in the driveway that day.

My husband finds dimes all the time. One of the most incredible dime stories was one when he was golfing. He was upset that day because the golf course reminded him of Randy. They had played golf there together. Well, he hit the ball way out in the rough. When he walked out to find his golf ball, there, sitting right next to it was a dime. It was sitting right on top of the grass, not buried or anything. He knew at that moment that it had to be Randy giving him a sign.

Another time, and this was it really, really something, I went down to the Florida Keys with a friend. We stopped at a beach for her to go snorkeling. I decided to walk along the beach while I waited for her. As I was walking along the beach, I started praying, 'Please Lord, send me a sign that Randy is with me.' Randy loved the Keys. I continued walking and talking to myself and then I saw some things that had washed up on the beach. It was obvious they had been there for a really long time. As I bent over to get a better look, I couldn't believe my eyes, right there on top of all the debris was a shiny dime. That was amazing.

I had another incredible experience. I was away on a cruise. It was the 11-month anniversary.

I was feeling really rotten, so I told my husband before we do anything I've got to find a church. We found a really old church in San Juan, Puerto Rico. I had brought a bunch of pictures of Randy and some of the other young people who had also died in our community. I was going to pray for everybody that day. I laid all the pictures on the railing and I also placed a special prayer on the altar. I began to pray. I prayed for a sign that they were all together and okay. No sooner had I spoken the prayer than a cool burst of air hit me in the face and blew all the pictures off the rail. They ended up together on the floor. The prayer remained on the altar but all the pictures had blown off.

I was in shock; I didn't know what had happened. I looked up to see where the air might have come from. It all happened so fast. I thought maybe the air conditioner had turned on. I didn't know what to think. My husband was behind me and he saw the whole thing. He asked me what had just happened, and I said 'Didn't you feel the cool air?' He said, 'No I didn't feel anything.' So I said, 'Maybe it's the air conditioner." He said, 'This is a very old church, there is no air conditioner in here.'

I've had many other experiences: a light around the crucifix, alarm clocks going off, horns going off, phone calls and bizarre things happening with the phone and bells in the house, as well as significant songs appearing on the radio. I've felt him around me so often. I've even had glimpses that appeared to be a trail of energy that followed his friend when he walked through the room. I've heard 'Mom', had doors open, and a lot of electrical stuff. He's been around me and I know he's okay.

On St Patrick's Day, Randy's friend came by to show me a tattoo he had put on in memory of Randy. I try to be here for him, because I know it's really hard for him still. When we started talking, I looked at his eyes. As I looked, his eyes turned into my son's eyes. I can't explain what it felt like. I was shocked, but it was really a nice feeling. I didn't want to keep staring and I didn't want to tell him what I was seeing because I didn't know if it would upset him. His eyes actually changed. His eyes were blue and Randy had brown eyes and dark hair, his eyes actually changed! I couldn't wait until he left so I could tell my husband. As soon as he left, I ran into the living room where my husband was sitting.

I said, 'I think I had a miracle happen,' and I started crying. I was crying not because I was sad, but because I was happy. I told him the story and he said, 'I saw the same thing.' I didn't know until a lot later that when that happens, it's known as transfiguration. Once you have one sign you want more and more and more and more. It was Elizabeth who kind of opened the door to help me believe all of this and look for it.

~ ~ ~

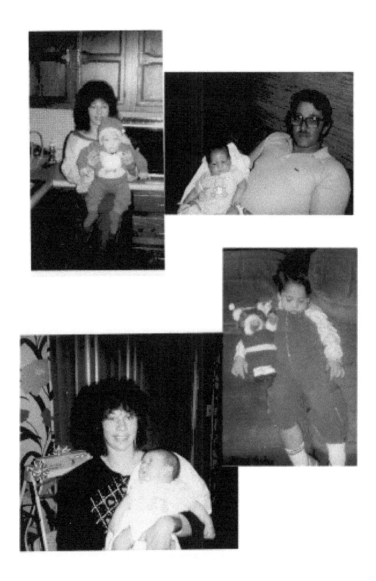

Leona and Randy with Randall as a baby

Valerie: (by the author):

About a year after Stephanie died I asked Valerie, Steph's mom, if she had heard from Stephanie.

When Shannon Andersen asked me if I had heard from Stephanie I told her I wasn't really sure. I wasn't convinced that I personally had heard from Stephanie but, there have been some incredible things that have happened. One is a dream that my nephew Jacob had. He was five at the time. Jacob loves attention. His Mom, Judy, says he's spoiled but he's just a delight. His eyes sparkle and he still has his shy smile.

I asked him about the dream he had, but he didn't talk openly about it – just said yes or no to my questions. Judy told me all about it. He said he saw Stephanie in his dream but she didn't talk to him. He knew he was in heaven because there were no cars and it was very beautiful with lots of children and animals, all playing together. He bent to pick up his cat, Rusty, who died shortly after Steph died, and when he stood up, he saw Stephanie across a street and she was smiling at him.

Then he said he went and sat on Jesus' lap and they talked. Jesus told him it was time for him to go and as he was leaving, he saw a man he didn't know. Later that day, he saw a picture in Judy's room. He pointed to it and said that was the man he had seen in his dream, only the man didn't have a beard in heaven. The picture was a photograph of Judy's brother Wayne, who committed suicide about 10 years ago.

When Judy told me about Jacob's dream, I was so thrilled because it confirmed for me that Stephanie was in heaven. I have been so concerned, scared really, to think that her spirit or soul might have gone to what one would envision as hell, or purgatory since that is what I'd been taught by my Catholic faith. Ever since Stephanie died, I have been reading voraciously, beginning with books about near-death encounters, moving on to books by psychics like John Edward, just to get a glimpse of what is said or understood about the spiritual implications of suicide.

Being raised a Catholic, I have vivid memories of the nuns talking about suicide and saying it was just the same as murder, a mortal sin that condemned the victim to everlasting hell. I even read in one of the psychic books that suicide is never an option and that the person's spirit went to a type of holding place, like the old Catholic purgatory, where the spirits shifted aimlessly and in despair until they somehow awoke, but, only after being there as long as they would have lived had they not taken their lives. I remember praying so fervently, and still do, that this was not Steph's fate. Jacob's dream helped me with that.

Steph does come to visit me on my way to work. She comes through songs. One day I heard 'The Heart Goes On' by Celine Dion, then I switched the radio to some of my CD's and for some reason, I felt that I should turn back to the radio and when I did, 'I Hope You Dance' was just coming on! I will always feel she's talking to me when I hear these songs. I also read the book 'Hello From

Heaven'. It's so good because it tells the stories of people who have been visited by loved ones who have died and who give them messages of love and encouragement. It reminds me of the 'messages' I've received, both directly and indirectly.

My most direct message was a dream, or I think of it as a vision, because it was so vivid and completely different from a dream. It was shortly after she died, maybe about a week, and I was dreaming that she was not feeling well and I was tucking her into bed (one of our favorite rituals). In my vision, I realized she was dead and said, 'Oh, boy, I'm going to miss this – what were you thinking?' She looked at me and said (telepathically), 'I wasn't thinking'. Then her eyes looked at me so intently and so lovingly that I felt waves of love. Her eyes were different, all dark brown and warm. It was so vivid I woke with a start. I shared this vision with a group of other parents in mourning. At the time all I could do was cry, so I'm not sure anyone understood what I was saying.

~ ~ ~

Patti: (as told to the author)

It was not long after our interview that Patti, Jason's mother, called me to say that after I left she'd gone into the laundry room and found a shiny new head's up penny. We had the same experience together when she came to the high school to make a safe driving video for the students. When I got in my car the next morning I looked down at the floorboard of my car and found another penny.

On the second anniversary of Jason's death, Patti's

mother had gone on the Internet and ordered butterflies to be released at the gravesite. The butterflies did not arrive as scheduled by Saturday evening. She told herself not to worry, believing it would all work out. She decided just to go with what we had planned, even though she was a bit disappointed. When they arrived at the cemetery, a green frog with a white stripe popped up from the white lei that were placed at the grave.

It was just hanging out on the bamboo cross that Jason's buddies had made!! He stayed the whole service and was there when we left…it was awesome. I have been there many times and have never seen a single frog. Pastor Bob was also impressed by the presence of this creature. Plus, the pure green frogs with the white stripe are very rare, so one friend informed me afterwards. Many reassuring things did happen that day and night.

~ ~ ~

Jason in Tahiti

❧❧❧❧ *Reflections by Elizabeth* ❧❧❧❧

I can't speak for other mediums or psychics but my experience of the spirit world is that there is no pain. They don't feel pain. As long as you work from your heart you can't harm anyone and that's where it comes from, my heart. It is a gift from God. I truly believe it is.

❧❧❧❧❧❧❧❧❧❧❧❧❧❧❧❧❧

Chapter 10

My Own Signs

I too have had many signs from my loved ones, far too many to recount; from dragonflies constantly flying into my house, to lizards and irises blooming on special dates, as well as hats along the highway and more....but my favorite stories are those that involve rainbows.

This started in 2002 when my daughter's young friend of whom I was very fond, died. The morning of the funeral there was a rainbow. About a week later we planned a memorial at a waterfront pavilion. I arrived early to set up the music and pictures. As I paused and looked out over the water, there appeared another rainbow! After that, whenever I was missing and thinking about him I would ask for a rainbow. During one week, between November 1 and November 7 of the year he died, I saw 22 rainbows! I do believe our loved ones do their very best, using very creative ways, to let us know they are okay.

Sometimes our grief is too intense to experience messages and signs from loved ones. Not everyone notices them (or perhaps they miss them), but, I believe our loved ones want us to know they are okay and they will go to extraordinary measures to reach us with the message of their survival, just as Jody did when he sent for Windy through Elizabeth Palin.

Like Patty, Jason's mother, I have had only one reading with Elizabeth. That was all I needed. That was not the only message I received through Elizabeth however. In fact, Elizabeth was the one who let me know my friend Joe had passed. That was an incredible example of how those on the other side can use Elizabeth to get a message to us.

On the day Joe died I visited the hospital. It was Monday, January 29. Joe had fallen into a deep sleep, the last stage of life. He stirred only slightly when I kissed his forehead, told him it was I, and whispered my last words, "Send me signs Joe; I'll be looking for signs." I left the hospital about 12:00 noon.

I was busy working the next day and Elizabeth was in Flagler Beach doing readings. I had arranged to pick her up and drive her to a group that evening. Elizabeth remembered Joe from a group that had met at my house. When I arrived she began to tell me about one of the people she had seen that day. "A man came in today. He said to give you a message. He said to 'tell Shannon Andersen thank you.'"

When she described him, I didn't know who it might be. "His friend died yesterday," Elizabeth went on, "and he came through in the reading." I still didn't make the connection. "His friend's name was Joe," she said, gently letting me know. I still didn't get it. "I think it was your friend." She finally said. "No," I said, "I was just at the hospital yesterday, someone would have called me. I'm sure they would have called me." "No," she said, "I'm sure it was your friend Joe." I still didn't want to believe. "Well, I'll call the hospital" I said still in denial.

I called the hospital. The operator switched me to the 3rd floor nursing station. "Is my friend still with us?" I asked. "No," she said, "He died yesterday." I was shocked, the first reaction we all feel. I'll always remember the last time I saw Joe alert. He was sitting on the side of the bed. His hospital gown was draped over his left shoulder, his body was browned and his head shaven, as he always had it. His dark eyes held a pool of wisdom. He looked just like a monk. Joe was a good man.

I tried to find out who the man was who had come for a reading and sent me the thank you message. He had been there just one day after Joe died. He would have had to have had an appointment for months. There was no way he could have known that Joe was going to succumb to his cancer when he booked the appointment. There is always a long waiting list to see Elizabeth. At the funeral I told a mutual friend about the experience. I thought she might have had an appointment and released it for one of Joe's brothers when he died. That was not the case. There was only one other explanation.

Months before, I had seen Michael, a friend Joe and I had in common. At that time we talked about "his good buddy Joe," and our shared respect and love for him. He asked me about the book I was writing about Elizabeth and I gave him her telephone number. "Don't tell me when you go," I told him, "and you can use any name you want because I want you to know for sure I had no contact with her." Her readings are so accurate often people can't believe she has no fore knowledge. I tell anybody who sees her the same thing. "You can use your middle name, your mother's maiden name, no name at all. Do whatever you need to do to assure yourself that what she is telling you is in fact coming from your loved ones."

I called our mutual friend and asked, "Could it have been Michael who had a reading with Elizabeth?" She told me she would find out. A few weeks later she called me. "It was Michael," she said. "Joe came through for him. In the reading Joe told him he was shocked. He didn't expect to die when he did. He said he still had a lot of loose ends and would be hanging around to make sure everything was taken care of." I was so happy to know that it was Joe himself who let me know (through Elizabeth and Michael) that he was okay!

~ ~ ~

Another time a young man named Tim brought a very special gift to his parents on his birthday. I had been working with his parents for almost a year. His father had lost all faith in a God who had been very precious to him. He no longer believed in life after death. I told Tim's parents about my experience with the 22 rainbows in one week and I encouraged them to ask their son for a rainbow on his birthday which was coming up.

I realized I was sticking my neck out, but somehow I knew their son wanted to bring them comfort. His birthday, August 23, fell on a Saturday. All day long I looked at the weather wondering if it was possible that these lovely people might receive a sign from their son. It was raining that day and at noon I went outside to look as I saw the sun coming out...but no rainbow. Later that day I was working on my computer when husband asked me to come outside to help him.

There was no rainbow in sight...but I still intuitively knew there had to be a rainbow. I felt it. I jumped in the car and drove the one mile to the beach. When I arrived I saw it begin to form across the sky over the ocean. Back into my car I leaped and rushed home. As I sprinted into the house I called out over my shoulder to my husband, "there's a rainbow."

I picked up the phone and called. Tim's mother answered in two rings.

"Hello Shannon," she said. "I knew it was you...

we saw it...! "

She went on, "I have to tell you my husband went out earlier looking for it. Shannon, I must ask you... what does it mean?"

I took a breath...

"I can only tell you what I think it means," I said. "I think it means your son says he's fine and he wants you to know how very much he loves you still."

~ ~ ~

In 2006 my father died. I had no need to seek a medium, not even Elizabeth. I already had proof from the time I'd spent with her. I know my father is fine and happy and continuing the next step we will all take one day. I no longer fear death. I do now believe, because of all that I have learned from this experience, that life is not an end but a beginning and death is a birth into the next chapter of an eternity.

I think about death every day, however. It is a part of my job at hospice. For me death has become merely our tomorrow, a next step, the future, and the loss is not a loss but merely, as grief expert Alan Wolfelt says, "a different form of a continuing relationship...." and while losses accumulate like rocks in a backpack, I've learned to insulate my heart with beliefs that nourish rather than pierce.

❧ Epilogue ❧

After working with hundreds of grieving people and numerous parents who have lost children to death, I've learned one thing that helps tremendously is a belief that allows for life continuing after death and the possibility of contact from the other side. Faith is often not enough. Sometimes faith without proof leaves those grieving empty and hopeless. There may be anger at God and the inability to find consolation through faith. When people feel a connection to their loved ones after death, when they experience irrefutable proof for themselves that their loved ones are safe and happy, one huge boulder is removed from the path of their grief journey and the light at the end of the tunnel becomes visible.

I can only thank Elizabeth Palin for helping my family and me in the early days of loss and for giving me the living proof that our loved ones are still with us. I want collectively to give thanks to the beautiful young ones on the other side who have diligently sent their love and messages of hope to those of us who remain behind missing them.

Thanks all you blessed angels. We love you and miss you...and we are still listening.

❧ About Elizabeth Palin ❧

Elizabeth is a world-renowned Psychic/Medium with a God-given ability to help grieving hearts. Born a Catholic in Liverpool, England, even as a young girl Elizabeth knew she had a gift. She took the mission of 'praying the souls out of purgatory' seriously - often leaving the entire altar ablaze with prayer candles. Rebellion ruled her teens; and although a young mother, she partied with the likes of the Beatles and Jerry and the Pacemakers. At this time a psychic told her she would become very well-known in America. She thought that was "Rubbish!" believing she would never leave England. However, after having a Near-Death-Experience as a result of alcohol poisoning, the ones who had 'passed over' began to appear on a regular basis, and within a few years, the psychic's predictions came true. Today Elizabeth lives and practices in Celebration, Florida, and thousands of people worldwide seek her counsel. She has been called the 'Lightgiver' because of her amazing talent. She owns her own production company, and has produced two DVDs: *Tarot –The Three Card Spread*, and *Elizabeth Palin – Lightgiver: Grief and Loss*. She is collaborating on a book about her life, *No Squares in the Universe.*

For more information go to
www.elizabethpalin.com

❧ About the Author ❧

L. Shannon Andersen is a hospice Bereavement Counselor and Transpersonal Life Coach. She practices as a licensed counselor in the state of Florida where she lives with her husband. She has spent years of study in religion, psychology, metaphysics and *A Course in Miracles*. She applies the knowledge gleaned from these sources in her writing.

Her first book, *The Magdalene Awakening: Heralding the Re-emergence of the Divine Feminine,* was published in 2006 and traces her spiritual awakening through After-Death Communications, past life regressions, synchronicity, and the discovery of a soul group returned with a link to Mary Magdalene and her message for today.

She was trained by Dr. Brian Weiss in past life regression therapy, and works with grieving individuals and others seeking to explore their spiritual origins. She is an international speaker doing workshops of a spiritual nature in New York and Hong Kong. Her professional credentials include training in hypnosis, Neuro Linguistic Programming (NLP) and certification as a Traumatologist working with individuals who have been affected by trauma or disaster. She is also a Compassion Fatigue Specialist working with other people in the helping profession with burn-out and is certified in Critical Incident Stress Debriefing (CISD).

Shannon loves to work with other counselors, nurses, doctors and other professionals to help them take care of themselves. Shannon took accredited life coach training from the Institute of Life Coach Training created by Dr. Patrick Williams, and she now offers transpersonal life coaching to a limited number of clients.

She has been published in the "Florida Journal of Public Health" and "Florida Living Magazine, featured in a 2002 issue of "Q Magazine", in Hong Kong.

~ L. Shannon Andersen, M.Ed., LMHC~

**To learn more about Shannon Andersen
and her other publications, visit her website
www.TheMagdaleneAwakening.com**

❧ **Bibliography** ❧

Carr, John Dickson, *The Life of Arthur Conan Doyle,* Carroll & Graf Publishers, New York, New York, 1949.

Cooke, Grace, *Minesta's Vision,* White Eagle Publishing Trust, Great Britain, 1992.

Gutenheim, Bill and Judy, *Hello from Heaven*, Bantum Books, New York, NY., 1997.

Kirkpatrick, Sidney D., *Edgar Cayce: An Amrican Prophet,* The Berkley Publising Group, a division of Penquine Putnam, Inc., New York, New York, 2000.

Kubler-Ross, Elisabeth, *On Death and Dying,* Scribner Classics, Kindle Ed. New York, N.Y., 2007.

Moody, Raymond, *Life After Life,* Bantum Books, Double Day Publishing Co. New York, NY. 1997

Notes

CPSIA information can be obtained
at www.ICGtesting.com
Printed in the USA
LVHW092229050322
712733LV00001B/2